CREOLE MOON PUBLICATIONS

CREOLE MOON PUBLICATIONS

MERRY CHRISTMAS

GUMBO YA YA KRAMPUS-SANTA HOLIDAY EDITION

Denise M. Alvarado, Editor

Contributors

Denise Alvarado
Bayou Basil
Carole Cusack
Carolina Dean
Celeste Heldstab
Melony Malsom
Mama Moon
Morgan St. Knight

Creole Moon Publications

Copyright 2015, 2016 by Denise Alvarado

All rights reserved. This book or any portion thereof may not be reproduced or used in any manner whatsoever without the express written permission of the publisher except for the use of brief quotations in a book review or scholarly journal.

First published 2015
First Printing: 2016

ISBN-13 (paper): 978-1541352728
ISBN-10 (paper): 1541352726

Library of Congress Cataloging in
Publication Data Available upon request.

Creole Moon Publications
P.O. Box 25684
Prescott Valley, AZ 86312
creolemoonpublications@gmail.com

Ordering Information
U.S. trade bookstores and wholesalers please contact:
Creole Moon Publications
creolemoonpublications@gmail.com

FROM THE EDITOR

Merry Christmas

Gruß vom Krampus !

It's that time of year for Yuletide festivities and the shenanigans of that jolly ole elf and his sidekick, Krampy Claws. I decided to focus this issue on these two characters who have taken many cultures by storm with their undeniable presence during the Yuletide season. Santa Claus, aka Saint Nicholas, aka Father Christmas, aka ad infinitum—is presented in my *Field Guide to Santa and Friends* in this issue. And Krampus, while not nearly as well-known in the United States as he is in Europe, is introduced in this issue as he becomes more popular as a star on the Silver Screen. In this issue, we explore the legends surrounding him and other fascinating cultural figures associated with the Yuletide season.

In addition to presenting more Santa and Krampus than is probably ever necessary, we have some other fun and interesting articles for you in this issue of Gumbo Ya Ya. We get a peek at Carolyn Morrow Long's yearly Christmas cards, Celeste Heldstab brings you a delicious recipe for prosperity cookies and Mama Moon shares some fabulous winter herbal remedies. Bayou Basil brings her *Homemade Herbed Petition Paper and Scented Love Ink* and Morgan St. Knight shares an insightful article called *Silent Night: Using the Dark Part of the Year to Brighten Your Life.* Melony Malsom brings us *Krampus: The Sordid Tale of the Christmas Demon* and we end the issue with a wonderful article by Carolina Dean called *Hoodoo for the Holy Days.* Of course, there are other articles and tidbits of information between articles and you will discover these surprises as you peruse the issue.

This has been a fun issue to put together for you and I sincerely hope you enjoy reading it. As always, if you have any comments, questions or requests about this issue or future issues, feel free to email me at creolemoonpublications@gmail.com.

Brightest blessings,

Denise Alvarado

Editor in Chief

Website: www.creolemoon.com
Blog: conjureart.blogspot.com
Facebook: facebook.com/gumboyayaezine
Official FB Fan Page:
facebook.com/AuthorDeniseAlvarado
Instagram: Instagram.com/creole_moon
Pinterest: pinterest.com/voodoomama

CONTENTS

From the Editor	6
Schnapps, Whipping and Sacks: How Christmas Traditions Evolved around the World by Carole Cusack	10
Krampus: A Review	18
More Krampus Media Blitz	24
Gloria En Excelsus Deo Greeting Cards by Carolyn Morrow Long	29
Prosperity Cookies by Celeste Heldstab	32
Winter Herbal Remedies by Mama Moon	34
Mistletoe	36
Solstice Incense	37
Homemade Herbed Petition Paper and Scented Love Ink by Bayou Basil	38
Krampus: The Sordid Tale of the Christmas Demon by Melony Malsom	46
A Field Guide to Santa and Friends by Denise Alvarado	56
Weird Santa Photos	102
Silent night: Using the dark part of the year to brighten your life by Morgan St. Knight	106
Holy Day Hoodoo by Carolina Dean	116
Image credits	122
Contributors	130

SCHNAPPS WHIPPING & SACKS

How Christmas Traditions Evolved Around the World

by Carole Cusack

Professor of Religious Studies, University of Sydney

Christmas has become a cultural event, associated with the giving of gifts and lavish meals with friends and family. But the traditional understanding of Christmas is that it's a Christian celebration of the birth of Jesus.

The idea of giving gifts may be traced to the Bible, in which the infant Jesus was presented with gold, frankincense and myrrh by the Three Wise Men, named in apocryphal texts as Caspar, Balthasar and Melchior. This received a boost in the Middle Ages, when Boxing Day, December 26, became a holiday when masters gave their apprentices and other employees "boxes" – that is, gifts.

Yet, the celebration of Christmas has distinct variations around the world. Some of these local traditions are very interesting and arise from particular historical circumstances.

The figure of Santa Claus, the jolly bringer of presents to good children, is derived from St Nicholas, a fourth-century Christian bishop of Myra. Two famous stories are told of him, that associate him with gifts and children:

1. He rescued three girls from a life of prostitution by giving their father three bags of gold for their dowries.
2. He brought back to life three young boys who had been murdered and pickled by an evil innkeeper.

Santa Claus has elves and reindeer as companions in general Western folklore. But in other traditions around the world, Santa's helpers are far less friendly.

The Netherlands: Naughty Kids are Taken to Spain

In the Netherlands, Sinterklaaas brings children presents on December 5 (the day before the feast of St Nicholas, December 6).

Dutch traditions say that Sinterklaas lives in Madrid, wears a red clerical robe and a bishop's mitre, and has servants called "Zwarte Pieten" (Black Peters). He arrives each year at a different port on November 11. Children prepare by leaving carrots for his horse and putting out a shoe for presents to be put in.

The Zwarte Pieten keep lists of the naughty children who receive pieces of coal rather than gifts. Very naughty children are put into sacks and taken to Spain as a punishment.

The reason Sinterklaas lives in Madrid is because between 1518 and 1714 the Netherlands was under the control of the Holy Roman Empire, at that time ruled by the Hapsburg Dynasty of Spain. Spain, therefore, meted out both punishments and rewards to the Netherlands (as the Zwarte Pieten and Sinterklaas do to Dutch children).

Though Zwarte Pieten are black because they spent so much time in chimneys, in the modern Netherlands many are concerned that they may be racist.

Central Europe: St Nicholas' Companion is a Sinister Creature that Whips Bad Children

In central Europe, including Austria, Bavaria and the Czech Republic, the companion of St Nicholas is the sinister Krampus, a terrifying creature with

(Continued on page 14)

Saint Nicholas and his servant, by Jan Schenkman (1850). Licensed under Public Domain via Wikimedia Commons.

fangs, horns and fur, who punishes naughty children by whipping them with sticks, called "ruten bundles". These whippings are intended to make bad children good.

Those who cannot be whipped into niceness are put into Krampus' sack and taken back to his den (somewhat akin to the Zwarte Pieten and Spain).

Also similar to the Zwarte Pieten is Krampus' gift of coal, though he also gives ruten bundles (sticks sprayed with gold paint displayed in houses all year round) to remind children to be good throughout the year.

Krampus has pagan origins and is claimed to be the son of Hel, the goddess of the dead in Norse mythology. The den to which he takes bad children is the Underworld, which literally means that if you are naughty you will die.

This pagan origin made the Christian churches in central Europe hostile to Krampus, in particular the Catholic Church, which banned rituals dedicated to him.

In the 21st century, as the influence of Christianity has receded, these traditions have been revived with great enthusiasm.

Groups of men dress as Krampus and rowdily parade through towns on Krampusnacht (December 5, before the feast of St Nicholas), drinking Krampus schnapps – a traditional fruit brandy brewed extra-strong for the occasion – and scaring children.

Some Krampuses bear more than a passing resemblance to Chewbacca, with horns! Krampus has now been immortalised in film, with *Krampus*, a horror comedy directed by Michael Dougherty, being released in 2015.

South Korea: a Family Occasion Where it's Fashionable to Attend a Christmas Church Service

South Korea has more Christians than many Asian countries and Christmas is a public holiday there, even though 70% of the population is not Christian. Christmas trees abound, decorated with twinkling lights and often with a red cross on the top. Lavish Christmas displays in shop windows are common. It's also a time of family celebration.

For many non-Christians, it has become fashionable to attend a Christmas church service, and groups of people walk through neighbourhoods singing Christmas carols.

Christmas cake (though not European-style fruit cake, but either sponge cake with cream, or ice-cream cake) is a popular seasonal indulgence. Christmas dinner, however, is firmly Korean and usually includes noodles, beef bulgogi and kimchi (pickled cabbage).

Santa Claus also features and is called Santa Kullusu or Santa Haraboji (Grandfather). He may sometimes wear a blue suit instead of a red suit, something that was common in the 19th century, when Santa Claus was often portrayed wearing blue or green, until red became the most popular colour.

Yet Christmas is not the great consumerist event that is common in the West; Koreans generally give one gift only to close friends and family.

New Year, which is a huge festival in all East Asian cultures, has far more extravagant celebrations. But Christmas is very popular with younger Koreans and is likely to become a larger part of cultural life in the future.

*This article was originally published December 21, 2015 on theconversation.com and is reprinted here with permission under a Creative Commons license.

THE CONVERSATION

Old Father Christmas, Forrester's Pictorial Miscellany for the Family Circle (1854). Licensed under Public Domain via Wikimedia Commons.

REVIEW: KRAMPUS

Denise Alvarado

Legendary Pictures' *Krampus*, presents a dark and twisted tale of the infamous creature of European pagan origin best known in the United States as the infernal sidekick of Saint Nicholas. Instead of greeting the holiday with the usual Christmas cheer, the movie presents a predictable plot where all hell breaks loose with a family punished for their dysfunction as Krampus stalks the nonbelievers and malcontents during a dark blizzard on Christmas Eve.

Krampus was co-written and directed by Michael Dougherty, known for another holiday-based horror film, *Trick 'r Treat*. *Krampus* begins with a portrayal of a normal family who is awaiting the arrival of extended family members to celebrate the holiday. Parents Tom (Adam Scott) and Sarah (Toni Collette), grandmother Omi (Krista Stadler), teenaged daughter Beth (Stefania LaVie Owen), and pre-teen Max (Emjay Anthony) anxiously await Sarah's sister Linda (Alison Tolman) and her family, a rude and crude bunch who display irreverence for the holiday and disrespect for themselves and others.

Linda's husband, Howard (David Koechner), is portrayed as a stereotypical redneck who loves guns and the Pittsburgh Steelers. Linda's family also includes a cranky aunt (Conchata Ferrell) and several obnoxious cousins. The ill-natured cousins taunt Max for still believing in Santa, and when they find and read the letter he wrote to Santa they further humiliate him, which results in one disillusioned little boy who turns his back on Christmas.

Max unknowingly casts a sort of spell on himself when he rips his letter up into tiny little pieces and scatters them to the winds. Consequently, a terrible storm arrives and the power for the entire town is lost. The remainder of the movie occurs fittingly in the darkness of a raging blizzard setting the stage for the arrival of the so-called demon Krampus who is ready to unleash his wrath on the family, forcing them to either unite or fall apart.

The film is not entirely serious; it is somewhat of a hybrid horror/comedy—sort of along the lines of *Gremlins*— which is what saves it, in my opinion. I have to admit I went into the movie already biased by the trailers I had seen that portrayed Krampus as a purely evil creature. The usual misrepresentation by the Big Screen regarding characters of pagan origin is beyond annoying. Nevertheless, I put that aside and watched the movie. I wanted to see how Krampus looked. I was also interested in any backstory—I wanted to see how they were going to present Krampus as a legendary figure. That the movie failed to achieve full horror or full comedic results did not bother me. I was, however, disappointed that most of the scenes with Krampus and the monsters occurred close-up or in suggestive ways, as opposed to giving the audience a good look at them so we could marvel at the creative handiwork. Sigh.

Still, *Krampus* does have some good moments.

A series of strange events begin to occur, but no one seems to know what is going on. No one, that is, except for the German grandma, Omi, who in the beginning keeps to herself what she knows. Later, she recounts her childhood memories of Krampus in a hauntingly beautiful scene that explains just how Krampus found the American family. Omi calls Krampus the "Shadow of Saint Nicolas" and shares how growing up in poverty made her dislike the holidays to the point that she summoned Krampus as a result. He, in turn, drug her parents into hell but spared her, leaving behind a brass bell as a reminder of the consequences for losing one's Christmas spirit.

Of course, hell is a Christian concept and has nothing to do with the actual pagan creature. I guess if Krampus is likened to the devil though, then hell has to figure in the rewritten mythology

> # CRITICS REVIEWS
>
> Critics reviews for Krampus are mixed, with the majority not loving the film:
>
> "*Krampus* isn't especially scary, but it generates goodwill nonetheless for treating its home-invasion-for-the-holidays setup with an appreciably straight face." Justin Chang for *Variety Magazine*
>
> "No one has been too naughty to be subjected to this reindeer poop." Stephen Whitty for *New York Daily News*
>
> "It's not exactly Gremlins quality, but this seasonal frightener does have a good dash of that film's anarchic spirit." Benjamin Lee for *The Guardian*

somewhere. I have lost all hope for Hollywood ever getting anything pagan correctly depicted.

Meanwhile, Krampus lurks about outside of the family home and upstairs in the attic a number of surprises await. Some presents that had been delivered earlier (by Krampus) start shaking, getting the family's attention who predictably go upstairs to investigate. There, they find der Klown-in-the-box who decides to eat one of Max's cousins. If that's not scary enough, they are taunted and attacked by Lumpy, Dumpy, and Clumpy, three evil gingerbread men. No, I'm not making this up.

But wait, there's more.

After fighting off the gingerbread demons, the family is attacked by three of Krampus' evil elf minions who end up kidnapping Dorothy, Howard, and the baby. The rest of the family make a run for it in the blizzard which proves to be a bad move as they are eaten by a snow monster. There are a few side plots of various family members being terrorized by the devilish Krampus crew but ultimately, the only one left alive is Max, who has to confront the Christmas demon alone. Krampus gives Max a bell like the one his grandmother was given, only this one was wrapped in a piece of Max's torn letter. Max apologizes to Krampus for losing his Christmas spirit and pleads for the return of his family, and though Krampus considers the request as he dangles Max over the pits of Hell, he drops him anyway.

Instead of landing in fire and brimstone, Max wakes up in his bed on Christmas morning as if it all was nothing but a dream. He gets out of bed and joins his family who are downstairs opening presents. Then, he opens a present that contains the Krampus bell and everyone suddenly remembers what had happened. They all sit dumbfounded while the camera pulls back and shows Krampus watching them from inside a snow globe on a shelf in his creepy lair.

There's no deep meaning behind the obvious in the movie: karma's a bitch when Krampus is watching.

As an artist, I would have loved to have seen more of the Krampus character. I particularly loved the (far too short) scene where the group of Krampuses waere walking in the snow. I also totally loved the little Krampus bell and would love to purchase one just because, if only the manufacturer wetanz.com would get them back in stock. Folks selling them on Ebay are selling them at nauseatingly inflated prices. For example, the actual cost from the manufacturer is $11.99 whereas Ebay sellers are pricing them at $79.00.

All in all, *Krampus* is not a bad movie, but it's not especially good either. It falls short in a number of areas and does not give enough visual effect to satisfy the artist or pagan in me. It left me hungry for more than a huge, refillable $7.50 bag of buttered popcorn could compensate for. Still, Krampus lovers should check it out for themselves. I've made that easy for you by providing the QR code that goes to the directly to the movie on Amazon.com where you can watch it for just a couple of bucks.

Scan the QR code with your IPhone or Android to watch the movie on Amazon.com.

Genre: Comedy, Fantasy, Horror
Rated PG-13
Runtime: 98 minutes
Release date: December 4, 2015
Director: Michael Dougherty

More Krampus Media Blitz

The 2015 release "Krampus" is not the only movie to have been made about Santa's evil twin. 2015 saw the release of *Krampus: The Reckoning*, and *A Christmas Horror Story*, both starring the legendary creature. 2014 brought the release of *Krampus the Christmas Devil* while in 2013, *Night of the Krampus* was released. In 2016, there is a film about Black Peter called *Silent Night, Bloody Night 2 Revival*. Finally, there is one obscure little film called *Santa Krampus* put out by Wormwood Studios that I couldn't even find a release date for but listed just for shits and giggles. I didn't even touch on the horror flicks starring Santa Claus, but a Google search will help you twisted folks find those. You can find trailers of these movies on Youtube and Amazon.com. Here's a break down of the Krampus films along with their ratings:

Krampus: The Reckoning (2015)

A strange child named Zoe has a not so imaginary friend in Krampus who is unleashed upon a small town and begins to wreak havoc on all the naughty

people to punish them at Christmas time. Ooh, scary.
Starring: Shawn Anderson, Amelia Haberman
Runtime: 1 hour, 28 minutes

A Christmas Horror Story (2015)

Not even Santa is safe in this movie. Evil befalls the small town of Baily Downs, leaving the community plagued with malevolent spirits, zombie elves and Krampus—the anti-Santa Claus. William Shatner fans should love this one.
Starring: George Buza, William Shatner
Runtime: 1 hour, 39 minutes

Krampus The Christmas Devil (2014)

When the Christmas Devil visits a small town to punish the naughty children, one police officer must hunt him

down before more kids end up kidnapped or murdered by the evil demon.
Starring: Jay Dobyns, Paul Ferm
Runtime: 1 hour, 23 minutes

Night of the Krampus (2013)

When kids in a suburb vanish in the weeks leading to Christmas, all evidence points to the existence of Krampus. It's up to a team of supernatural investigators to solve the mystery, save the children, and face the night demon. Description from IMDB.com
Starring: Khristian Fulmer, Erin Lilley
Runtime: 26 minutes

Silent Night Bloody Night 2: Revival (2015)

After a death in the family, siblings Angelica and James Zacherly travel to the small town of East Willard on Christmas Eve to pay their respects.

They stay at a homely bed and breakfast where they learn the legend of Black Peter, Santa Claus' vengeful brother. But when they find the lost journal of Jeffrey Butler, they discover the town has its own sordid history - one more rooted in reality. Description from IMDB.com
Starring: Julia Farrell, Jennifer Runyon Corman
Runtime: 1 hour, 30 minutes

Santa Krampus

At Christmas, some believe in Santa Claus, and some in Krampus. Yet what if they are both right, and it is a spirit that can cause good and chaos? A new holiday horror film from writer director Jerry Williams (Purvos, UFO Crash in Kentucky, Monsters of the UFO). Description from IMDB.com
Starring: Steve Guynn, Ford Windstar, Cherokee Hall, Kenny Bates, Heather Scream Price, and Todd Burrows.
Runtime: 27 minutes

GLORIA IN EXCELSUS DEO

Greeting Cards by Carolyn Morrow Long

Denise Alvarado

Every year, author and former conservator of paper artifacts and photographs at the Smithsonian Institution, Carolyn Morrow Long, designs some very cool greeting cards and sells them as limited edition during the holiday season. This year, Carolyn calls her card "Gloria in Excelsis Deo" and this is what she had to say about them:

> Every year I make a collage for the Winter Holidays and have it reproduced as a card. I sell them and keep some for my own use.
>
> This year I have a new card, "Gloria in Excelsis Deo," with Jacques-the-Cat looking up into the sky at the angels. Twenty are going to the Ogden Museum of Southern Art in New Orleans, and I hope to sell some at the DC Authors Festival in which I'm participating.

Last year's collage card was "Welcome Yule," reproduced from a collage created by Long. The collage incorporates images of a porcelain Santa Claus and polar bear figurines, a Mexican cut-tin moon, reindeer, rabbits, felt stars with smiley faces, a stuffed Santa, antique block letters, and of course, Krampus. Carolyn shared some thoughts about what influenced that design:

> Yule is a European pre-Christian winter solstice festival. The solstice, December 21, is the short-

est day and longest night of the year, after which the days begin the lengthen until the summer solstice on June 21. Yule celebrates the rebirth of the sun and the return of the light. In 336 AD, the celebration of the birth of Jesus became conflated with Yule and other solstice festivals when December 25 was designated as Christmas day. Pre-Christian traditions of decorating the home with candles and evergreens, feasting, wassailing, singing, and gift-giving were incorporated into Christmas.

St. Nicholas, a fourth-century Christian bishop who performed many acts of charity, became known as the patron of children. Over time he has morphed into the present-day figure of Santa Claus, who rides through the night sky in a sleigh drawn by reindeer bringing gifts to good girls and boys. In some European countries, Santa Claus is accompanied by Krampus, a devilish being who chastises naughty children with his bundle of switches and leaves them lumps of coal instead of treats.

If you are interested in purchasing some of Carolyn's unique Christmas cards, you can inquire with her directly on Facebook at the start of the Christmas season each year: facebook.com/carolyn.m.long.1

PROSPERITY COOKIES

From the Kitchen of
Celeste Heldstab

These cookies are made whenever there is a time of need or to assist a friend. A perfect cookie for the holidays with the added bonus of a little prosperity magic in the ingredients!

Ingredients (makes 5 dozen)
- 4 c. all purpose flour
- 3/4 tsp. baking soda
- 3/4 tsp. Ground Ginger
- 1-1/2 tsp. Cinnamon
- 1-1/2 tsp. Ground Cloves
- 1/2 tsp. Salt
- 1 c. unsalted butter, softened
- 1-1/4 c. sugar, plus more as needed for coating
- 1/2 c. molasses
- 2 eggs
- 1 tsp. vanilla

Preheat oven to 350*F. Sift together the flour, baking soda, spices and salt. Set aside. Cream the but-

Remember to always stir clockwise...

ter with the sugar, until fluffy, about 3 minutes. Beat in the molasses and mix in eggs one at a time. Stir in the vanilla. Add the dry mixture in three parts, mixing well after each addition. Put extra sugar on a plate and coat walnut-sized dough lumps with the sugar. Place 2 inches apart on an un-greased cookie sheet, and press each cookie down slightly with a fork. Bake for 14 minutes, until light golden.

Remember to always stir clockwise, if blending by hand. A mixer will automatically spin clockwise. Keep warm, and positive thoughts in your mind while making these cookies. They will fill your home with a wonderful smell, and be sure to share some of your cookies with others. To pass prosperity onto others is a blessed thing to do.

WINTER REMEDIES

Mama Moon

Winter, that time of year when everyone is walking around coughing and sneezing and passing whatever they have around. I always hated going to the local pharmacy and trying to figure out which cold medicine I needed to unstuff my nose. So, I came up with wonderful aromatherapy oil that I can add to a diffuser and feel better. In fact, it's so good at keeping winter illnesses away that I use it all winter long. What is it you ask? Well, here you go...make a big batch so you can use it all winter.

- Ravansara
- Clover Bud
- Cinnamon
- Lavender
- Eucalyptus
- Vitamin E oil
- Your favorite carrier oil

I usually use 1 ounce of each of the oils and mix them all into a large bottle. Add 1 ounce of carrier oil and 10 drops of vitamin E oil. If you mix less, then adjust the carrier oil and vitamin E also.

Need a cough syrup? Try this. Get yourself cherry bark and marshmallow roots. Put them into a pan and cover with water. Bring to boil in a pan then simmer for about ½ hour. Strain the herbs out into a jar and add honey. Mix it up and you have a great tasting cough syrup.

One of my favorites is elderberry brandy. It's so easy to make. You'll need elderberries and a cheap brandy. Fill a large jar with elderberries about 3/4 full. Pour the brandy into the jar, but keep the brandy bottle. Close the jar and shake it. This takes 4 to 6 weeks to brew so make sure you shake it every day. After about 4 to 6 weeks, strain the elderberries out and pour the brandy back into the bottle. If you want, you can mix in some honey, too. You're done! Keep it in the frig to use whenever you need an immune boost, or sip some every day.

Now go out and enjoy winter and be healthy!

Hand and Body Cream

Is your skin dry and itchy in the winter? Or do you suffer from dermatitis or other skin issues? Well, here is a great cream to try:

- 1/4 cup Shea Butter
- 1/8 cup Coconut oil
- 5-10 drops of Cedarwood essential oil
- 5-10 drops of Lavender essential oil
- Vitamin E

Mix all together for a hand/body cream for rashes.

MISTLETOE

The legend of kissing under the mistletoe has it roots in a Scandinavian myth. Legend has it that the Norse God, Baldur was protected from evil by everything that came from the elements of fire, water, air and earth. But an evil spirit formed an arrow from mistletoe and killed him. The tears of Baldur's mother, Frigga, became the white berries of the mistletoe. His life was restored and Frigga, being the Goddess of Love and Beauty, is said to have kissed anyone passing under the mistletoe. The myth of mistletoe spread throughout the land and even enemies would call a truce when they met underneath it.

SOLSTICE INCENSE

Incense Recipe

Solstice Citrus Incense
Denise Alvarado

Combine the following ingredients and burn on charcoal or place out in a bowl as potpourri for a delicious holiday fragrance. Store in a glass container.

- 1 tbsp. dry orange peel
- 1 tbsp. star anise
- 1 tbsp. cloves
- 1 tbsp. dry tangerine peel
- 1 tbsp. pine needles
- 1 tsp. orange essential oil
- 1 tsp. lemon essential oil

HERBED PETITION PAPER

Bayou Basil

Here is a recipe for making homemade herbed petition paper and scented red love ink. You will need the following ingredients for making paper pulp:

- 3 gallon bucket (like the ones from the hardware store)
- Mortar & Pestle
- 12 quart stainless steel pan
- Rubber Gloves
- Wooden Spoon
- Metal sieve
- Cheese cloth
- Blender
- Caustic Soda (Lye)
- Laundry Starch

For making paper, you will need:

- Large plastic dish basin

- Wooden frames with strong netting stapled tightly
- Extra wooden frame without netting
- Newspapers or towels

Preparing the Pulp

Fill the 3 gallon bucket with all the fresh herbs and flowers that you need for your desired petition. You'll want to cut the herbs and flowers fairly small (approximately 2 inch pieces). Crush the thicker pieces with your mortar & pestle to speed up the breakdown process.

Put 1 quart of water into the 12 quart stainless steel pan. Add 2 tablespoons of lye and stir with wooden spoon. This is where the rubber gloves come in; lye gives off strong fumes and can burn the skin so make sure the room is well ventilated. If any splashes up on you, rinse with cold water immediately. Now, add the herbs and flowers to the pan. Add a little extra warm water to cover, if necessary. Mix well and cover. Simmer on low for approximately 1-2 hours, or until the fibers are broken down and soft.

Drain the mixture and rinse thoroughly to remove any lye residue. Then, strain pulp through the metal sieve.

At this point, the pulp will be reduced in size. You are going to want to put all the pulp into the cheesecloth and take turns rinsing and squeezing out all the water. Do this for several minutes.

Now, you are going to blend together approximately 2-3 tablespoons of the pulp with 3 cups of water, for about 20 seconds. The finer the plant fibers, the finer the paper will be. At this point, the pulp can be used as is, or you can add it to recycled paper pulp to thicken. Since you are going to be writing on the paper, it will need to be treated beforehand with laundry starch. To do this, simply add about ¼ of a teaspoon of laundry starch to a bit of water, mix and add to the pulp. To make recycled paper, simply take old paper, tear it up into tiny bits and soak overnight in warm water. When ready to use, blend approximately 2 ½-3 tablespoons of paper pulp with 3 cups of water for about 15 seconds and then add in the laundry starch as you did above.

Making the Paper

First, make sure that any dried herbs or flowers, which you'd like to show up on your paper are nearby and ready for use. I also sometimes add a drop or two of oil related to the work I am doing to the paper at this stage.

Fill the plastic dish basin with the pulp. Stop about 1 inch from the top. Put the unscreened wooden frame over the screened wooden frame.

Hold them together firmly and dip vertically into the basin. Once all the way under the water, turn it so that it is horizontal. Raise the frame straight up, slowly. Keep the frame horizontal while bringing it out of the water. Put the frame on top of laid out newspapers or towels to dry. Now is the time to add the dried herbs, flowers, and/or oils. Remove the empty top frame and sprinkle the bits that you want on the top and let the paper dry completely. When it is fully dry, carefully lift the edges to peel the paper off of the screen. Sometimes you need a thin spatula or putty knife to help lift the paper. It is now ready to use!

Make sure to clean the frames between each use. I made a bunch of frames so that I can make a bunch of paper at once.

Scented Red "Love" Ink

You will need:

- 1oz each of dried lavender flowers, lemon verbena, rose, geranium, rosemary, and sweet myrtle leaves.
- 1 cup poppy petals (fresh)
- Water
- Small pot
- Jar
- 15% Isopropyl alcohol
- Cheesecloth

Put all herbs and petals in the pot. Add water until just covered. Bring to a boil, then cover and simmer for approx. 30 minutes. Add extra water as needed. Make sure the water does not fully evaporate, but reduces. Turn pot off and allow to steep, covered, overnight. Strain through cheesecloth, directly into jar. Add just a splash of alcohol to preserve. Give a little shake. It is now ready to use!

Santa Claus as illustrated in Puck magazine by Frank A. Nankivell, (1902). Licensed under Public Domain via Wikimedia Commons.

TEAM KRAMPUS VS TEAM SANTA

Drinks Schnapps, whips naughty children, and leaves birch bundles in their homes.

Likes milk and cookies, lets kids sit on his lap, and gives them nice presents and treats for being good.

Have you been NAUGHTY or NICE?

If you are wondering how the holidays will go for you, remember karma's a bitch when it comes to Krampus!

KRAMPUS

The Sordid Tale of the CHRISTMAS DEMON

Melony Malsom

Twas the night before Saint Nicholas Day, and all of the good little children are sleeping and nestled in their beds. At least they hope they have been "good" that year, as they bury their heads beneath their bed covering, breathing heavily and glancing worriedly at the shadows outside their windows. A floor board creaks and little ones close their eyes tight as they wait to feel cold, clawed fingers grab their tiny ankles and drag them out from beneath the safety of tightly wrapped blankets—kicking and screaming into the darkness—all the while wishing they had never fought with their siblings or shaved the fur off the cat. This is NOT story most of us associate with the season of Yule and Christmas. In fact, here in the U.S., we enjoy tales of dancing sugar plums as we bask in the warm, comforting twinkle of a decorated tree.

(Continued on page 48)

Krampus parade in Pörtschach am Wörthersee. Photograph by Johann Jaritz (2013). Licensed under CC BY-SA 3.0 via Wikimedia Commons.

Most children go to sleep on Christmas Eve feeling confident that they will wake to find a stocking brimming with treats and a plethora of gifts beneath the tree. Well, grab some eggnog and get uncomfortable because this is the tale of *Krampus, the Christmas Demon*.

The story of Krampus cannot begin without first giving a brief overview of his jolly, gift-toting partner. Saint Nicholas dates back to the fourth century AD. He was a very kind and humble man who earned his sainthood from his consistent acts of kindness and charity towards his fellow man. Saint Nicholas died on December sixth, 345 AD.; the memory of his kind works, however, lived on throughout the centuries. Stories of Saint Nick became such an integral part of the Yule and Christmas season that he has become the poster-boy for the season itself. He is jolly old St. Nick, Santa Claus, Father Christmas, Kris Kringle, Papa Noel, Jule Nisse, Sinterklaas, and Odin The Wanderer, to name a few and like the season of Yule itself, his roots lie within Pagan beliefs.

Parents throughout time have taught their children that to be *nice* and do good deeds will earn them gifts and rewards, while being *naughty* will get them nothing but punishment and sorrow. This parental tactic isn't always successful, especially with most mischievous children, and bringing in an empty shoe or boot containing only a rod, void of any treats, coins, or gifts on Saint Nicholas' Day only seemed to make their behavior worse. What was a European parent to do with an ill-behaved, rambunctious child? Surely, they couldn't taint the sacred image of Saint Nick; he was a Saint, after all. Santa had to have a cohort, an accomplice, a companion to traverse the world by his side, a sort of *good, cop-bad cop* of the holiday season. The German people were just the folks to give him one. Enter Krampus, the Anti-Claus.

Old card reading *Gruss vom Krampus* (*Greetings from Krampus*). Licensed under Public Domain via Wikimedia Commons.

His name derives from the German word *Krampen* meaning *claw*. He is a vile, black (although sometimes depicted as red) demon with horns, mismatched feet with cloven hooves, bristly hair, and a long, red tongue. He bares likeness to the fabled Satyr and Fauns of Pagan fertility mythology. He is the Christmas devil who takes great delight in punishing all of the horrid little children that refuse to listen and respect their elders.

Some of the earliest tales of Krampus appear in the Fourth Century C.E. and originate from a Germanic, Pre-Christian Pagan culture in the Alpine region of Austria. Some of these Germanic tribes fled to this secluded, mountainous region when the onslaught of Romans began converting the people to Christianity; hence, keeping some of their Pagan beliefs alive and well. It is true Krampus rode shotgun to Saint Nick, delivering justice and punishment where ever it was needed throughout Europe. His visage may have started in Austria and Germany, but he was soon adopted by Switzerland, Croatia, Italy, and France. Krampus begins his seasonal trek of searching out all of the naughty children every year on December fifth, *Krampusnacht,* or *Night of Krampus.* Children would place a shoe or boot outside the door and if they had been little angels all year, the next morning on *Nikolaustag* (St. Nicholas Day), they would retrieve them to find them filled with treats and gifts. However, if they had indeed been naughty, they would find only a piece of birch rod in the shoe which meant Krampus would soon be coming for them. We can only imagine what might have occurred had the legend been true. That night, as the good little children slept soundly, without a care, the naughty

(Continued page 52)

Krampus and St. Nicolas by Unknown. Licensed under Public Domain via Wikimedia Commons.

A modern Krampus at the Perchtenlauf in Klagenfurt. Photograph by Anita Martinez (2006). Licensed under CC BY 2.0. via Wikimedia Commons.

children would fret far into the night and for nights after, never knowing when HE might come for them. First, they might hear the clicking of cloven feet upon the streets and walkway outside their windows. The door to their room might slowly creek open, revealing a horrific silhouette as a hellish stench invades their nostrils. Before they can utter a word, he appears by their bedside, leering down at them with contempt and anticipation. The children are dragged, beaten bloody with thorny birch rods, and stuffed into a basket Krampus carries upon his back. They are taken away to his lair, some accounts say to Hell itself, and crammed in cages or chained. Sometimes the children are returned, sometimes not. If this bedtime story didn't frighten the children into behaving, the tales of Krampus's punishments got worse. He would pull children's hair and rip out pigtails, lead children off cliffs, pull their ears, put them in shackles, drag them down to a lake of fire, and my favorite, drowning them in ink and pulling their lifeless bodies out with a long pitchfork. Many of these lovely holiday images appeared on a series of post cards throughout Europe in the 1800's with the title, "Gruss Vom Krampus" or "Greetings from Krampus." Krampus has proven himself very resilient through the ages. He has not only transformed the holiday season in Europe but is now gaining popularity in America as well. In many places, people have begun partaking in a rowdy celebration known as Krampuslauf or Krampus Run. On December fifth, folks basically dress up like devils, wild men, and witches, get intoxicated, and run amuck through town, terrifying the children and adults alike with their erratic, beastly behavior.

People weren't always so accepting of 'Old Nick' as he is sometimes affectionately called. During the 1930's, the Nazis, of all people, sided with the Catholic Church in outlawing Krampus and any celebrations thereof. Anyone caught dressing in his likeness would be arrested on the spot. Still, our beloved Christmas Demon persevered. Over time, Krampus has taken on different roles and imagery. A red demon with a black tongue, a black demon with a red tongue, a demon with a human face, mismatched feet, sometimes a hoof on one and a human foot on the other. Whatever his image, we can all agree that the story of Krampus makes the holiday season far more interesting, exciting, and a bit creepy. His influence to transform brats into well behaved children proves a lot more intimidating than, "be good or Santa Claus will leave you a piece of coal." I think the world's modern, over-privileged children could learn a thing or two from the birch rod of a Christmas Demon.

Season's beatings from Krampus to you!

References

Krampus: Home of the Christmas Devil. Krampus.com. Web 2011

National Geographic, *Who is Krampus? Explaining the Horrific Christmas Devil,* by Tanya Basu, 2013

Krampus at Morzger Pass, Salzburg (Austria). Multi-license with GFDL and Creative Commons CC-BY-SA-2.5 via Wikimedia Commons.

A FIELD GUIDE TO SANTA AND FRIENDS

Denise Alvarado

There are as many versions of Santa Claus and his sidekicks as there are cultures that celebrate Yuletide. *Saint Nicholas, Father Christmas, Sinterklaas, Jule Nisse, Jouluppukki—* these are just a few of the names for which he is known. What may surprise you is that Santa Claus has not always been a jolly ole elf or even humanoid. In fact, he has been depicted as an evil gnome, as well as a goat! And as for his sidekicks, well, they are arguably more interesting than St. Nick. From the Netherlands' white horse called *Schimmel* to the donkey of France and the Angels of Czechoslovakia, the companions of St. Nicholas run the gamut from beast to celestial being to human thug, from benevolent helper to scary monster. Whatever their form and demeanor, St. Nick's companions travel alongside him to help him get the job of gift-giving done.

(Continued page 58)

Nikolo by Jurij Šubic. Licensed under Public Domain via Wikimedia Commons.

Santa and Krampus, best buds.

Many of Santa's companions are as legendary as St. Nicolas himself due to their outlandish roles and character traits. Some are depicted as walking animals or humans dressed in black wearing an air of bedlam. Most are grounded in European traditions and in many respects, serve to provide the yang to Santa's yin. Whereas Santa is almost universally known as the good guy, his companions typically represent the opposite of Santa's benevolent nature, punishing children for bad behavior as opposed to rewarding them for good. They are not necessarily evil as it often seems; rather, they serve an important social role in controlling behavior through the threat of consequence. Known in German as *Kinderschreckfigur* or *child terror figures*, they scare the bajeesus out of little kids, promoting good behavior through threat and intimidation. Read more about the many faces of Santa and his curious Christmas companions.

The Field Guide To Santa & Friends

Belsnickel: A Yuletide peeping Tom with a penchant for spanking naughty children, Belsnickel is an old man in the woods who dresses in fur and peers into the windows of homes until he is invited in. Once inside, he asks the children if they have been good and if they pray. If they lie when answering him, he whips their bottoms with his switch. If they are honest and tell him they misbehaved, he only whips their knuckles. Belsnickel came to the United States with German immigrants and became a custom in Pennsylvania Dutch communities and other areas of the country with substantial German immigrant populations.

Ded Moroz: Ded Moroz, also known as Father Frost and Grandfather Frost, is the Slavic equivalent to Santa Claus. He is accompanied by his fairy grand-

Ded Moroz Illustration by Ivan Bilibin from the Russian fairy tale *Morozko*. Licensed under Public Domain via Wikimedia Commons.

daughter *Snegurochka*, also known as the *Snow Maiden* or *Snowy*. The beautiful companion of Ded Moroz sets him apart from his other European counterparts.

Russia's official Patron Saint and giver of gifts during the winter was Saint Nicholas. His physical depiction is based on the ancient legendary figure of Russian folklore, *Morozko*. It is this same legendary figure upon which Ded Moroz derives. According to legend, Morozko was nice to hard-working folks, but did not take kindly to mean, lazy people.

Interestingly, Ded Moroz is tied to Russian political history when he was banished during the Bolshevik Revolution in 1917. Apparently, he was viewed in a religious context as a children's god, and at the time the Russian government forbade any type of religiosity. Twenty years later, however, he began to appear during New Year's celebrations with Snegurochka. Together, they showed up on New

"As You Meet the New Year, So Will You Spend It"

A Russian tradition for reeling in the New Year is expressed in the title above. To leave or resolve all old debts in the old year and not carry them with you into the New Year, they say to wear brand new clothes in the lucky colors of the year to come. Also, it is believed that any wish made on New Year's Eve is sure to be fulfilled when done according to tradition. To do so, make a wish as the clock strikes midnight by writing your wish on a piece of paper, burning it in the flame of a candle, mixing the ashes in a glass of champagne and drinking it before the clock stops chiming.

Reference
http://lastochka-fromrussiawith-love.blogspot.com/2009_12_01_archive.html

Year's Eve to leave presents for children under the fir tree.

It is believed that Ded Moroz resides in a log cabin located in the Taiga forest where three rivers merge in the charming town of Veliky Ustyug in the Vologodsky Region of Northern Russia. According to Russiapedia.com, Ded Moroz spends his summer days there reading letters sent from kids all over the country with their requests for gifts they hope to find under the New Year's Tree the next January 1st. See *Snegurochka*.

Father Christmas: The personification of Christmas, British in origin. Generally believed to have derived from an old English folkloric tradition that centered around adult merry-making, singing and feasting, Father Christmas was known during Medieval times as *Captain Christmas, The Prince of Christmas* and *the Christmas Lord.* The first known English personification of Christmas, however, was in a carol published in the mid 1400s attributed to Richard Smart, who refers to him as *Sir Christemas.* In the carol, Sir Christemas announces the birth of Jesus and encourages his listeners to drink: "*Buvez bien par toute la compagnie,* Make good cheer and be right merry, And sing with us now joyfully: Nowell, nowell" (Simpson and Roud 2000).

When Puritans took control of the British government in the mid-1640s they made concerted efforts to abolish Christmas and to outlaw its tradi-

Father Christmas with holly crown and wassail bowl, the bowl now being used for the delivery of children's presents (1879). Licensed under Public Domain via Wikimedia Commons.

tional customs. The celebration of Christmas in England was forbidden. During this time, the Pamphlet writers of the Royal Court began to link Father Christmas with the lamentation of the good ole days of merriment and cheer. He was often characterized in a negative light as being popish, sad, and pitiful. Several pamphlets described Christmas as being on trial, such as the anonymously written *The Arraignment, Conviction and Imprisoning of Christmas* (1646) and *The Examination and Tryall of Old Father Christmas* (1658) written by Josiah King. Upon the Restoration in 1660, Josiah King reprinted his 1658 pamphlet with additional material presenting Father Christmas in a better light: "[he] look't so smug and pleasant, his cherry cheeks appeared through his thin milk white locks, like [b]lushing Roses vail'd with snow white Tiffany ... the true Emblem of Joy and Innocence" (Wikipedia contributors N.D.).

Father Christmas as a legendary character was maintained throughout the 18th and 19th centuries largely through Christmas folk plays known as *mummers plays.* Up until Victorian times, Father Christmas had no associations with gift-giving and children, only with adult feasting and merrymaking. As Victorian Christmases began to focus on family and children, Father Christmas began to change to be consistent with the holiday. It was at this time he began to be a bringer of gifts who descended down the chimney and filled stockings with goodies.

When the American Santa Claus made his appearance in England in the 1850s, Father Christmas began to take on some of his characteristics. By the 1880s the nocturnal bringer of gifts was known as Santa Claus and as Father Christmas. By the twentieth century, any distinction made between the two figures had faded away.

Hans von Trotha: A German knight born into the aristocratic family Trotha. He is infamous for his

(Continued on page 66)

Hans Trapp by Almanach de Wintzenheim - knarf.info. Licensed under CC BY-SA 3.0 via Wikimedia Commons.

well-known feud with Henry, Abbot of the Order of Benedictine monks at Weissenburg Abbey. During the feud, Hans von Trotha built a damn to cut off the water supply to the lands in question, which he later tore down in response to complaints by the abbot. This resulted in a flood that devastated the town of Weissenburg economically. For eight years, the knight engaged in open warfare against the abbot. When he would not cease from his hostilities even when told to do so by the Emperor, he was summoned to appear before the pope. However, he refused to go in person and instead wrote a letter to the pope in which he professed his faith to the Church but also accused the pope of engaging in unethical and immoral behavior. As a result, von Trotha was excommunicated from the church and following the custom of the day, he suffered an imperial ban. People who fell under the status of an imperial ban were considered legally dead and were subject to being robbed, injured or killed. Anyone who perpetrated a crime against a banned person could do so with impunity.

Following his excommunication and imperial ban, Hans von Trotha became a local legend known as *Hans Trapp* or the *Black Knight* (*Schwarzer Ritter*) in the Palatinate region. Over time he was described as a robber baron and associated with cannibalism, the Devil, and the dark arts. He was even associated with a local legend concerning a nearby spring called the *Legend of Jungfernsprung*. The most common version of the legend comes from local author, August Becker (1857):

> Once a young maiden ventured into the Forest of Dahn to pick berries. When she was far away from home, a man suddenly burst out of the thicket, probably the robber baron, Hans Trapp from Berwartstein Castle. The man clearly intended to rob the virgin of her innocence. So the young maiden gathered up her skirts and took to flight, but the villain came ever closer to her. In her panic, the young lass failed to watch where she was going. All of a sudden she found herself, panting for breath, at the edge of the precipice with the houses of the town far below. Without stopping to think, the young maiden fell over the abyss. And now the miracle happened: because her skirts ballooned out and let her float down gently, she survived the leap entirely unhurt. And ever since, at the spot where her foot landed, a spring has flowed.

In Alsace at the time of Saint Nicholas, Hans Trapp began to appear alongside the saint as his nightmarish sidekick who scared little children into behaving. How this leap came to be made in unknown; but, it appears he was used as a regional substitute for *Knecht Ruprecht*, who was Saint Nicholas' usual companion in Germany at that time.

Jezšek: Translates as Baby Jesus, who in the Czech tradition is the one who has been delivering presents during Christmas time for centuries. No one knows what he looks like, and there is some debate as to whether he is the Baby Jesus or an adult Jesus who brings the gifts. He usually comes during Christmas Eve after everyone leaves the room where the Christmas tree is located. While the children wait in their rooms for him to arrive, the parents put gifts under the tree, and when they are finished, they ring a bell and quickly slip out of the room. The children rush into the room hoping to catch a glimpse of Jezšek which they never get, of course, and so he remains relegated to the realm of Christmas mysteries.

Jlasveinarnir (Yule Lads): In Icelandic folklore, *Jlasveinarnir* or *Yule Lads*, or *Yulemen*, are thirteen trolls who have become the modern day (almost) equivalent of Santa Claus. The Yule Lads are known as everything from pranksters to cannibals; but, mostly they are known as thieves, and most commonly as food thieves. The Yule Lads are traditionally said to be the sons of the mountain-dwelling trolls *Grýla*, the Child Eater, and her third husband *Leppalúði*. Grýla is said to be a monstrous ogre who comes down the mountain thirteen days in advance of Christmas in search of naughty children to put into her cauldron to boil and eat. According to lore, she is only allowed to take naughty children, and if they repent, she must release them. The Yule Lads also descend from the mountain in search of naughty children, but not all at once. Only one comes down the mountain each day— in a specific order—and stays for thirteen days. Each Yule Lad is associated with a specific trait which is reflected in their name, and they are all often depicted with the Yule Cat, the Yuletide beast who eats people who do not receive new clothes for Christmas.

The first Yule Lad to descend from the mountain is *Stekkjarstaur,* whose name has been translated as *Sheep-fold Sneaker, Sheep-cote clod, Sheep Pen Clod, Gimpy, Sheep-fold Stick,* and *Sheep Harasser.* He comes down on December 12 and stays until December 25. He loves sheep's milk but has a hard time getting it due to his peg legs or stiff legs. His specialty is harassing and scaring sheep and stealing them when he can catch one.

The second Yule Lad to descend is *Giljagaur,* meaning *Gully Gawk* or *Gully Oaf.* Prior to the advent of milking machines, he hid in gullies, waiting for an opportunity to sneak into the cowshed and skim the milk froth from the pails of milk. He descends on December 13 and returns December 26.

Stúfur, meaning *Stubby* or *Shorty,* comes down the mountain on December 14 and stays until December 27. He is abnormally small and steals pans to eat the scraps of food left in them.

Þvörusleikir, meaning *Spoon Licker* or *Ladle Licker,* steals *Þvörur* to lick, a type of a wooden spoon with a long handle used for stirring. He is said to be extremely thin due to malnutrition. He descends from the mountain on December 15 and stays until December 28.

The fifth Yule Lad to descend from the mountain is *Pottaskefill*, meaning *Pot Licker* or *Pot Scraper*. He comes on December 16 and stays until the 29th, during which time he busies himself stealing leftovers from pots that have yet to be washed.

Askasleikir, or *Bowl Licker*, descends from the mountain on December 17 and stays until December 30. He hides under beds waiting for someone to put down their bowl which he then steals, devouring what is left inside and licking it clean.

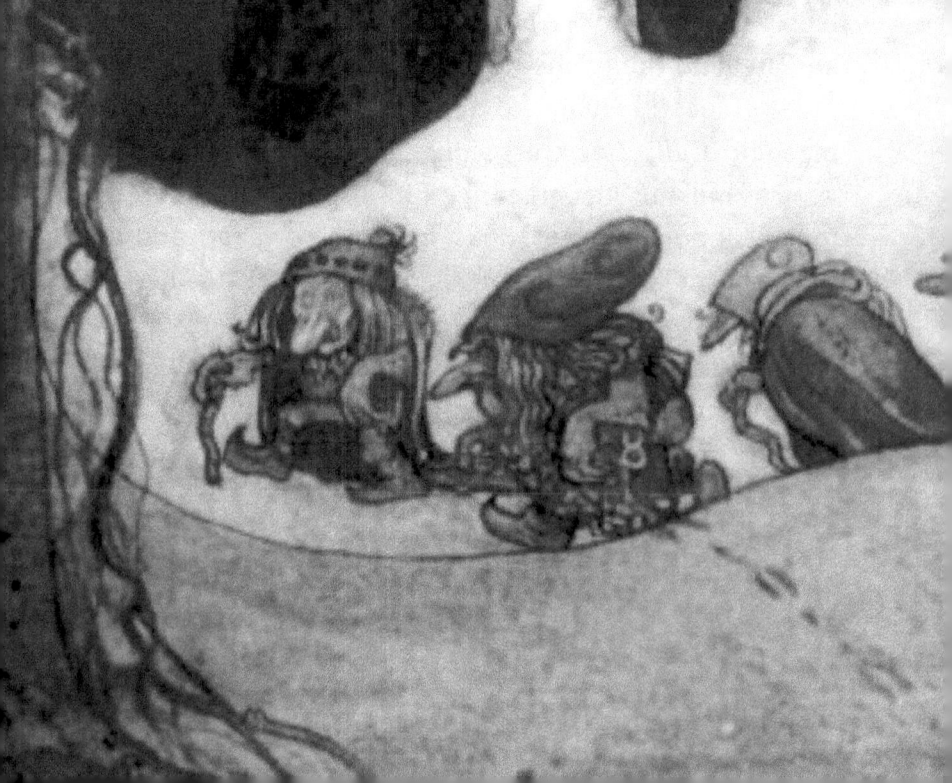

The seventh Yule Lad to descend from the mountain is *Hurðaskellir* or *Door Slammer*. As can be expected, he enjoys doing what his name implies—slamming doors, especially at night to keep people wide awake. He arrives on December 18 and returns on December 31.

On December 19th, *Skyrgámur*, or *Skyr Gobbler* or *Curd Glutton*, descends from the mountain. Skyrgámur loves to eat *skyr*, which is an Icelandic cultured dairy product similar to yogurt. He returns to the mountain on January 1st, presumably after getting his fill of skyr.

The ninth Yule Lad to descend from the mountain is *Bjúgnakrækir*, meaning *Sausage Swiper*, *Sausage Snatcher* or *Sausage Pilferer*. He hides in the rafters and snatches sausages that are being smoked. In fact, he loves sausages so much he steals them from wherever he can find them. He arrives on December 20th and returns on January 2nd.

Gluggagægir, meaning *Window Peeper,* peers through windows looking for things to steal such as toys he takes a fancy to. He arrives on December 21 and returns on January 3rd.

Gáttaþefur, meaning *Door Sniffer,* descends from the mountain on December 22nd and stays until January 4th. He is said to have an enormous nose and an acute sense of smell which he uses to locate *laufabrauð* or *Leaf Bread.* Leaf bread is a traditional paper-thin, fried bread decorated with leaf-life patterns that is eaten during the Christmas season. He also loves the smell of cakes and biscuits being baked for Christmas, snatching a few for himself whenever the opportunity arises. Here is a recipe for Icelandic Leaf Bread, the sort Door Sniffer loves to eat.

Laufabrauð - Icelandic Leaf Bread

- 2 lbs flour
- 1/4 teaspoon Baker's Ammonia (also known as ammonium bicarbonate or hartshorn)
- 1 teaspoon Salt
- 3 pints milk
- Fat for deep frying

Heat the milk just to the boiling point. Sift the flour together with the Baker's Ammonia and the salt. Stir the milk into the flour mixture and knead into a tough dough. Then, form the dough into a long roll. Cut the roll into pieces and roll out very thin on a well-floured surface. The bread is formed with a round dish and then traditional decorative patterns are carved into the dough with a sharp kitchen knife. If you google the term "Icelandic Leaf Bread" you will find images of the patterns. As each piece is completed, place between linen towels to prevent drying. Deep fry on high heat, decorated side down, until golden-brown. Before the leafbread cools too much, press down on it with a *laufabraudshlemmur*, a wooden board with a handle to flatten it. Some folks use two wooden cutting boards to achieve the same effect. Serve with butter or margarine. Note that baking soda may be used in place of Baker's Ammonia, however the latter is known for its effectiveness in baking crispy breads and pastries.

The twelfth Yule Lad to descend from the mountain is *Ketkrókur,* meaning *Meat Hook* or *Meat Snatcher.* He arrives on December 23 with a hook and steals meat of all kinds until January 5.

The last Yule Lad to descend from the mountain is *Kertasníkir*, meaning *Candle Stealer.* He follows children in order to steal their tallow candles presumably because they are edible. He arrives on December 24th and stays until January 6.

Originally, the Yule Lads were portrayed as being mischievous criminals who enjoyed harassing the population at large. They were depicted as

Folk depiction of Father Christmas riding on a goat by Robert Seymour (1836). Licensed under Public Domain via Wikimedia Commons.

scary creatures; but, in modern times, the Yule Lads have become much more benevolent. They have taken on some of the characteristics of Santa Claus, particularly his manner of dress and gift-giving. Nowadays, little children in Iceland place their shoes in their bedroom windows for thirteen days prior to Christmas. Each night, the Yule Lad that descended from the mountain that day leaves a special gift in the shoe. If, however, the children have been naughty, they get a rotten potato instead of a gift.

Jouluppukki: Finnish name for their Christmas Santa. Literally translated as *Yule Goat*, this was either an ugly creature of pagan origin that frightened children or an invisible spirit that helped with Yuletide preparations. Now, Yule Goats are available as cute little straw ornaments for the unsuspecting.

In Finland the Yule Goat is the bringer of gifts. In the past, the Jouluppukki roamed the streets on midwinter night creating a scene, begging for beer, telling dirty jokes, and scaring children. They also demanded presents instead of giving them out. By the nineteenth century, the Jouluppukki brought gifts to the upper class, and by the twentieth century, the Jouluppukki had morphed into a Santa lookalike. Sometimes, the Joulupukki is depicted as a goat-man on Christmas Eve. In some parts of Finland today, there is the custom of dressing up as a goat in order to get leftover food after Christmas.

Joulupukki and his wife, *Joulumuori* (*Old Lady Christmas*), live and work in Korvatunturi (Ear Mountain), in Lapland. Joulumuori has never been seen and apparently has nothing to do with Christmas. Joulupukki's assistants, called *tonttu* or *joulutonttu,* are human dwarves who don relatively drab attire and sometimes ride goats. Joulupukki differs from Santa Claus in that he visits people's homes and hands out gifts during the day when everyone is awake. Traditionally, he rings the doorbell of the front door of the home, and his first question is "Are there any good children here?" See entry *Yule Goat.*

Jule Nisse: The Jule Nisse is a mythological creature from Scandinavian folklore typically associated with the winter solstice and the Christmas season. It is a small being resembling the popular garden gnome, generally described as being no taller than 35 inches, having a long white beard, and wearing a conical knit cap in a bright color, usually red. Although physical descriptions are clear, nissen (plural) are usually invisible to humans and are known to use magic. The nisse is the Norwegian version of the Swedish *tomte.*

According to tradition, the nisse is an ancestral spirit, believed to be the soul of the first inhabitor of the farm where he resides. As such, he functions as a guardian spirit of the homestead. He lives in the burial mounds on the farm, but may also live inside the home or barn. He is associated with farm animals and has a particular fondness for horses. He often has a favorite horse on the farm that can be easily identified because it is exceptionally healthy and well-cared for. Often its mane and tail are braided. If one of these horses is observed, its

(Continued on page 78)

Jultomten by John Bauer (1911). Licensed under Public Domain via WikiArt.

braids should never be undone or else misfortune will befall the home.

Nisse should always be treated well so that he will do his job well, help out with chores, and protect the home and family from evil and misfortune. When insulted or ignored, nissen are known to be short tempered and tricksters, driving people crazy, stealing things, and even harming and killing livestock. There are some reports of Nissen actually biting people when they get angry. It is an extremely unfortunate thing to be bitten by a nisse as their bite is said to be poisonous. Healing from a nisse bite can only be accomplished through supernatural means.

Nisse are believed to bring prosperity and abundance to the household due to the work they do for the farmer and family. However, if a farm seems to be doing much better than their neighbors, they may become the target of the rumor mill due to jealousy. People may accuse the farmer of having a nisse who is stealing from them and doing the work of the devil. The resulting gossip can be quite hurtful and damaging to the farmer's livelihood. A farmer accused being helped by an ungodly being can be shunned by the community, much like it was in the past during the witch craze. In fact, during and after the Christianization of Scandinavia, the nisse and tomte suffered from being demonized. In a famous 14th century decree (*Revelationes*, book VI, ch. 78), Saint Birgitta warns against the worship of *tompta gudhi* (*tomte gods*). It was believed that to have a nisse or tomte in your home meant you had to engage in nonChristian rituals to keep them there and that your soul was at risk.

When I lived in Norway as a teenager, we were told to leave a bowl of oatmeal with a pat of butter on top outside for the Jule Nisse on Christmas Eve. This would make him happy and he would leave gifts. This tradition is not unlike the American practice of leaving milk and cookies out for Santa.

Apparently, Christmas is not the only time to leave nisse a bowl of porridge, though. Giving him porridge is seen as a type of offering or payment, perhaps for favors needed. It is believed that if the nisse does not receive his payment, then he will get very angry and become mischievous by doing things like tying cows' tails together, turning objects upside-down, and smashing things.

In the interest of keeping the Jule Nisse happy, I have provided you with a recipe for his favorite Yuletide porridge.

Jólagrautur - Icelandic Yule Porridge

- 1/2 pint water
- 3 pints milk
- 6 oz rice
- 1 teaspoon salt
- 2 1/2 oz raisins
- Cinnamon and sugar

- Milk
- 1 almond

Heat water to a boil, stir in the rice, and cook for ten minutes. Add the milk to the pot and cook over a low heat for one hour. Add the raisins in the last ten minutes. Add salt to taste. Add milk, sugar, and cinnamon to taste. For a Christmas custom, place a skinned almond in the pot. Whoever finds the almond should receive a small gift.

Knecht Ruprecht: *Farmhand Rupert* or *Servant Rupert* is a companion of Saint Nicholas as described in German folklore. In certain places in Austria, Knecht Ruprecht is an assistant to Saint Nicholas whose job it is to keep a watchful eye on him during his journey. According to German tradition, however, Knecht Ruprecht played a primary role as gift-giver and punisher in the distant past. During Yuletide, he would ask children if they can pray. If so, he gave them apples, nuts, and gingerbread. If not, he either beat them with a bag of ashes or gave them rocks and lumps of coal. In later lore, as a companion of St. Nicholas, well-behaved children received sweets from St. Nicholas while naughty children received coal or stones from Knecht Ruprecht. He may have also left switches in their shoes for their parents to whip them with. In all versions of the lore, Saint Nicholas and Knecht

Knecht Ruprecht und das Christkind, by unknown. 19th century. Licensed under Public Domain via Wikimedia Commons.

Ruprecht are accompanied by a variety of krampuses.

Krampus: Krampus is believed to have Pagan origins; though, his exact lineage is unclear. Some suggest he is the son of Hel in Norse mythology while others suggest he is similar to the satyrs and fauns of Greek mythology. The word *Krampus* originates from the Old High German word for *claw* (*krampen*). In German folklore of the Alpine region, Krampus is represented as a sort of Christmas devil complete with horns and cloven hooves. One of the Companions of St. Nicholas found in Eastern European traditions, Krampus wanders the streets in chains and bells punishing children who have misbehaved. He is commonly referred to as the "antiSanta" because he essentially represents the polar opposite of St. Nicholas.

Krampus Night or *Krampusnacht* occurs on December 5th, which is the eve of the feast of St Nicholas. Krampus is offered Fruit Schnapps or Peppermint Schnapps. While Santa dispenses gifts for the good children, Krampus is the bearer of coal and Ruten bundles. Ruten bundles are birch twigs sometimes painted gold and tied together. Krampus is known to carry the ruten bundles and to periodically swat misbehaving children with one of the twigs. Sometimes, he carries a whip for the same purpose. Krampus presents ruten bundles to families who leave them out as a reminder throughout the year for children to mind their manners and behave themselves.

Le Pre Fouettard (The Whipping Father): Remember the previous edition of Gumbo Ya Ya #4 that featured the story of *St Nicholas, Bringer of Gifts and Reanimator of Corpses?* Well this guy, *Le Pre Fouttard*, meaning *Whipping Father*, is said to be the horrible butcher who chopped up those three boys. According to the story told in 1150, the butcher lured three seemingly wealthy boys who were on their way to enroll in a religious boarding school. Along with his wife, he killed the children in order to rob them. One gruesome version tells that they drugged the children, slit their throats, cut them into pieces, and stewed them in a barrel. St. Nicholas discovered the crime and resurrected the children. After this, Le Père Fouettard repented and became St. Nick's partner. A slightly altered version of this story claims that St. Nicholas forced Le Père Fouettard to become his assistant as a punishment for his crimes. He now appears as a sinister figure dressed in black who accompanies Saint Nicolas and whips children who have behaved badly. Creepy.

Odin the Wanderer: Germanic in origin; a pagan god that rode an eight-legged horse named Sleipnir that could apparently fly or leap great distances. I want a horse like that...

Seriously though, numerous parallels have been drawn surrounding the figure of Odin, a major god amongst the Germanic Peoples prior to their Christianization. Odin is perhaps the most well-known god of Norse mythology who presided over Valhalla and is associated with war, sovereignty, wisdom, magic, shamanism, poetry, and the dead. He is described as a wanderer who took long solitary walks seeking and giving wisdom, and he spoke only in prose. He is equally as well-known for his shamanic journeys, these being documented in the *Ynglinga Saga* records and the Eddic poem *Baldur's Dreams*. As a god of war, Odin relished in the act over the purpose, and as such, is closely aligned with beserkers, for whom he had a fondness. As a ruler, he engaged in magic and cunning, and was fueled by inspiration, knowledge and the pursuit of power.

Odin, along with Freya, is the foremost Divine practitioner of the Germanic magical tradition *seidr*. Seidr is a woman's tradition, though many men practiced it also. To do so openly, however, left one open to ridicule and accusations of effeminacy. The fact that Odin openly practiced seidr as a god did not protect him from being subject to such scorn. He was controversial for many reasons and in Pre-Christian Northern Europe, practicing seidr made him appear to be unmanly and unfit to rule by others.

One of Odin's greatest contributions was the conscious creation of the runes. He is described as having "sacrificed himself to himself" by hanging on the world-tree Yggdrasil for nine days and nights. This description of sacrifice indicates he died a ritual death in order to receive the power he received, as is customary in shamanic traditions. During this time, he did not eat or drink, and became aware of the runes and the mysteries they contained.

How Odin became associated with Santa Claus or St. Nicholas is based on a few things. First is the obvious appearance of the old man with a long white beard. More importantly however, is the Wild

(Continued on page 86)

Odin, the Wanderer by Georg von Rosen (1886). Licensed under Public Domain via Wikimedia Commons.

Hunts Odin led in the sky during Yuletide with his eight-legged horse Sleipnir. According to the *Poetic Edda*, Sleipnir could leap great distances, just like reindeer. Children would leave their boots on the windowsill or by the chimney filled with carrots and hay to feed his magickal horse. This tradition progressed to Odin leaving gifts of nuts, fruits and sweets in their boots when he flew by. As Europe became Christianized, these beliefs became conflated with the Christian Christmas and St. Nicholas tradition, and St. Nicholas was ultimately bestowed with the gift-bringer trait.

Papa Noel: Papa Noel is the New Orleans version of Santa Claus. Like other manifestations of Santa, Papa Noel takes on decidedly regional Cajun characteristics. For example, he gets around in a pirogue, a narrow, flat-bottomed boat that can penetrate the deepest swamp, instead of a sleigh. His sleigh is drawn by eight chubby alligators and a red-nosed loup garou, as opposed to eight tiny reindeer led by Rudolf and his glowing red nose. Others say the alligators are just close friends, the loup garou is a distant cousin, and it's Papa Noel who has the red nose from drinking too much egg nog, Ponche au Lait, and Reindeer beer. Bonfires are lit all down the levees to help guide Papa Noel to the children in the area and they light up the swamp so his alligators can see while delivering all those gifts to the boys and girls along the bayous.

If you would like a red nose from drinking too much of Papa Noel's eggnog, then try your hand at making this old New Orleans recipe taken from *Camille Glenn's Old-Fashioned Christmas Cookbook.*

Papa Noel's Infamous New Orleans Egg Nog

- 12 large eggs, separated
- 1 cup sugar
- 1/2 cup Jamaica rum
- 2 1/2 cups best quality bourbon
- 3 cups heavy or whipping cream
- 1 cup milk
- 1 to 1 1/2 cups heavy or whipping cream, whipped
  freshly ground nutmeg, for serving

Combine the egg yolks with 1/2 cup sugar in a mixing bowl and beat until the mixture is creamy and thick. Add the rum and bourbon and beat thoroughly. Add the cream and milk and mix again.

Beat the egg whites until they hold a soft peak. Gradually add the remaining 1/2 cup sugar, beating until the whites hold a stiff peak. Fold them into the yolk mixture. Chill thoroughly until serving time. Pour the eggnog into a chilled punch bowl and gently fold in the whipped cream. Grate nutmeg over the top and serve. Makes about 30 small cups. Consume right away while the egg nog is thick and creamy.

Santa Claus. The Americanized version of St. Nicholas. Santa Claus is said to be a fictional folklore figure who is brings gifts on Christmas Eve, Christmas Day, or on his feast day, December 6. The main concept of Santa Claus seemed to become mainstay after the publication of the poem *A Night Before Christmas* in 1823. In this poem he is depicted as a chubby individual with eight tiny reindeer. According to Caitlan Green (2015) from the website, *The History of Santa Claus and Father Christmas:*

> The American Santa Claus is generally considered to have been the invention of Washington Irving and other early nineteenth-century New Yorkers, who wished to create a benign figure that might help calm down riotous Christmas celebrations and refocus them on the family. This new Santa Claus seems to have been largely inspired by the Dutch tradition of a gift-giving Sinterklaas, but it always was divergent from this tradition and was increasingly so over the course of the nineteenth and twentieth centuries. So, the American Santa is a largely secular visitor who arrives at Christmas, not the 6 December; who dresses in furs rather than a version of bishop's robes; who is rotund ra-

ther than thin; and who has a team of flying reindeer rather than a flying horse. At first his image was somewhat variable, but Thomas Nast's illustrations for *Harper's Illustrated Weekly* (1863-6) helped establish a figure who looks fairly close to the modern Santa. This figure was taken up by various advertisers, including Coca-Cola, with the result that he is now the 'standard' version of the Christmas visitor and has largely replaced the traditional Father Christmas in England. The image of Santa Claus as a benevolent character became reinforced with its association with charity and philanthropy, particularly organizations such as the Salvation Army. Volunteers dressed as Santa Claus typically became part of fund raising drives to aid needy families at Christmas time. (Green 2015).

Saint Nicholas of Myra: Primary inspiration for the Christian figure of Santa Claus and arguably the most popular saint in all the world—second only to the Virgin Mary. He was the Bishop of Myra in Lycia in the fourth century and died on December 6, 345 or 352. Before he was a saint, Nicolas was well-known for his generosity and gift giving. It is said he would secretly put coins in the shoes of those who left them out for him, and he would routinely help the hungry and the needy. He was a true philanthropist. Because of his generous nature and penchant for giving gifts, he became the role model for the modern day Santa Claus.

In Gumbo Ya Ya #4, I wrote a feature article all about St. Nicholas, so I refer readers to that article. Following is a small excerpt from that article:

> In Nicolas' time, people were appointed to sainthood by the unanimous consent of the people, typically based on their exceptional deeds, miracles performed, and martyrdom. In addition to those miracles already described, St. Nicolas is known for performing many other miracles. Aside from his skill as reanimator of corpses, he was able to calm stormy seas by blessing the waters, making him patron saint of mariners and fishermen. He became patron to prisoners and lawyers when he personally intervened to prevent three innocent men from being executed. And if that is not enough, he is also said to have multiplied the grain on a ship in sufficient quantities so as to alleviate a widespread famine. According to Le Saux (2005), "A ship was in the port at anchor, which was loaded with wheat for the Emperor in Constantinople. Nicolas invited the sailors to unload a part of the wheat to help in time of need. The sailors at first disliked the request, be cause the wheat had to be weighed accurately and delivered to the Emperor. Only when Nicolas promised them that they would not suffer any loss for their considera-

tion, the sailors agreed. When they arrived later in the capital, they made a surprising find: the weight of the load had not changed, although the wheat removed in Myra was enough for two full years and could even be used for sowing" (Le Saux, 2005). This latter miracle solidified St. Nicolas' patronage to chemists, bakers, and the hungry. (Alvarado 2013).

Sinterklaas: The Dutch version of Santa Claus; a historical figure with legendary, and folkloric origins based on Saint Nicholas. He is also known by the Dutch names, *De Sint (The Saint)*, *De Goede Sint (The Good Saint),* and *De Goedheiligman (The Good Holy Man)*. Sinterklaas is depicted as an elderly man with long white hair and a long white beard. He wears the iconical red robe and bishop's hat, carries a gold ceremonial staff and traditionally rides a white horse named *Amerigo* (in the Netherlands) and *Slecht Weer Vandaag*, meaning *Bad Weather Today* (in Belgium). Sinterklaas carries *The Book of Sinterklaas*, a big red book that identifies who has been naughty and who has been nice that year. His sidekick is the controversial Svarte Piet (*Black Peter*) who dons a black face. (see *Svarte Pete*).

Snegurochka: An essential part of the Russian New Year's celebrations and a helper to *Father Frost* aka *Ded Moroz* (see entry *Ded Moroz*). Her origins lie in

Slavic pagan beliefs when she was considered to be the daughter of Father Frost and the Snow Queen. In modern times, she is considered to be the granddaughter of Father Frost as opposed to the daughter. Traditionally, Snegurochka wore white clothes and a silver crown adorned with pearls.

According to another Russian fairytale, she was made out of snow by an old man and woman who regretted not being able to have children:

> In winter they made a girl out of snow. The snow maiden came alive and became the daughter they never had. They called her Snegurochka. But when the summer sun began to warm the land, the girl became very sad.
>
> One day she went into the woods with a group of village girls to pick flowers. It began to get dark and the girls made a fire and began playfully jumping over the flames. Snegurochka also jumped, but suddenly she melted and turned into a white cloud.

In some parts of Russia, there remains an ancient tradition based on her lore and the transition from winter to spring that consists of drowning a straw figure in the river or burning it on the bonfire to dispel the winter.

Whatever her true origins are, Snegurochka is always depicted as extraordinarily beautiful, with

(Continued on page 94)

Vasnetsov Snegurochka by Viktor M. Vasnetsov (1990). Licensed under Public Domain via Wikimedia Commons.

snow white skin, sky-blue eyes, and cherry red lips. She is forever young, always smiling, and travels with Father Frost on a horse-drawn sled to visit children and hand out presents. She often acts as a mediator between the children and Father Frost.

Originally, Snegurochka is said to reside deep in the forest. Today, she is said to reside in the Russian city of Veliky Ustug. She continues to be depicted as the most beautiful of all Russian folk characters. She wears blue, red, white or silver and her crown is sometimes replaced by fur-edged embroidered cap (Russiapedia.com). A search on Pinterest reveals some of the most strikingly beautiful art dolls constructed in her likeness I have ever seen. See *Ded Moroz.*

Svarte Piet (Black Peter): The sidekick to the Dutch Santa Claus, *Sinterklaas.* Svarte Piet is depicted in the controversial black face giving rise to current accusations of a racist tradition. A number of reasons are given for his black face, however, that reportedly have nothing to do with race: 1) it is said he has a black face due to the soot in the chimneys he crawls in and out of in order to deliver presents to children for Sinterklaas, 2) it disguises the true identity of the person playing the part, and 3) traditionally Zwarte Piet is said to be a Moor from Spain. Nevertheless, the figure of Zwarte Piet is considered by some to be racist in today's world of political correctness and/or institutional racism. As such, holiday traditions of Sinterklaas and Svarte Piet have been the subject of numerous protests and debates.

Like St. Nicholas and Krampus, Sinterklaas and Zwarte Piet are typically depicted carrying a bag which contains candy and presents for nice children. Svarte Piet tosses the candy about, supposedly reminiscent of the legend of St. Nicholas when he threw bags of gold through the windows of three girls in order to save them from a life of prostitution. Sinterklaas rides his white-grey horse over the rooftops at night, delivering gifts through the chimney via Svarte Piet to the well-behaved children. Svarte Piet carries a chimney sweep's broom made of willow branches for spanking naughty children and a jute bag for kidnapping them and taking them back to Spain. See *Sinterklaas*.

Svaty Mikuláš: In the Czech Republic, St. Nicholas or *Svaty Mikulš* is accompanied by the *Cert* (Devil) and *Andel* (Angel). Angels lower Svaty Mikuláš down from heaven on a heavy golden cord with a basket of apples, nuts, and candies. On the eve of St. Nicholas Day—December 5—a procession marking the beginning of the Christmas season is formed by Svaty Mikulš, an Angel and the Devil. Svaty Mikulš is there to give gifts to the children, the Devil is there to take the naughty children away, and the angel is there to protect the children from the Devil. According to the website stnicholascenter.org:

> The streets are filled with devils rattling chains, St. Nicholases with white cotton beards, long robes and bishops' staffs, and angels with paper wings on their way to visit small children in their homes. Traditionally, St. Nicholas quizzed children on the prayer-book and the Bible. Today, however, the questions are mostly about the previous year's behavior. The angel writes a record for each child in a large book and the children sing or say a poem to the saint. The devil rattles his chains, threatening to carry bad children off, but the angel, with a gold star on her forehead and dressed in a white gown, protects the children. Good children receive stockings filled with tangerines, nuts, chocolates, and small gifts. It is said that bad children get old potatoes or coal in theirs. Parents and other relatives also give a St. Nicholas gift, which may be hidden so children must hunt to find it. After the children's treats, St. Nicholas shares a toast with the parents. (stnicholascenter.org).

Tomte: See *Jule Nissen.*

Yule Cat: The Icelandic *Jólakötturinn* or *Jólaköttur,* is a character from Icelandic folklore believed to be traced back to the 19th century making it a rela-

Swedish Gävle goat (Gävlebocken) by Baltica (2003). Licensed under Public Domain via Wikimedia Commons.

tively new aspect of Scandinavian lore. The Yule Cat is also known as the house pet of the troll Grýla and her sons, the Yule Lads.

Depicted as a huge, vicious cat who roams the winter countryside around Christmas time, it is said that people who do not receive new clothes for Christmas are destined to become offerings for the Yule Cat. This belief was used as an incentive by farmers to ensure their workers finished processing the autumn wool before Christmas. Those that worked hard were rewarded with new clothes, but those who did not got nothing except the expectation of being consumed by the monstrous kitty beast. The Yule Cat as man-eating beast was popularized in part by the poet Jóhannes úr Kötlum in his poem *Jólakötturinn*.

Yule Goat: The Yule Goat is one of the oldest Scandinavian and Northern European Yule and Christmas symbols. In Finland, he is called *Jouluppukki*. Pagan in origin, one could argue the Yule Goat is the most popular of the animals associated with Yule.

The origin of the Yule Goat is suggested to be in its association with the Norse god Thor who rode through the sky in a chariot drawn by two goats named Tanngrisnir and Tanngnjóstr. It has also been suggested its origins lie in the old Scandinavian agricultural practice of bundling the last sheaf of corn from the harvest. The bundled sheaf was attributed with magical properties as the spirit of the harvest and was saved for Yule celebrations. Among other names, the bundled sheaf was called *julbocken* (the Yule goat).

Traditions associated with the Yule Goat varied according to region, though there were similarities among cultures. In Finland, the Yule Goat was a scary creature that demanded gifts from people.

During the 19th century, however, its role shifted towards becoming a gift-giver when men in the family started dressing up as the Yule Goat. Prior to this time, youths would go from house to house during Christmas time to perform small plays or sing Yule Goat songs, with one youth in the group dressed up as the Yule Goat. Another popular tradition was to sneak inside a neighbor's house and place a Yule Goat there (presumably one made of straw) without being noticed. That family in turn, if the prank was successful, had to get rid of the Yule Goat in a similar fashion. The Yule Goat tradition was eventually replaced with the Jultomte and Julenisse (Santa Claus) at the end of the 19th century

Today, the Yule Goat is best known as a Christmas ornament made out of straw and bound with red ribbons. Large versions of this figure are frequently constructed in towns around Christmas time and are often set on fire. The Gävle goat was the first of these goats, and remains the most famous Yule Goat as well as the most burnt down. See *Joulupukki.*

References

Alvarado, Denise. "Saint Nicolas, Bringer of Gifts and Reanimator of Corpses." *Gumbo Ya Ya #4*, Creole Moon Publications. 2013. Print.

Green, Caitlin. "America and the Creation of Santa Claus: A Guide." *The History of Santa Claus and Father Christmas*. Caitlin Green. 2015. Web. 23 November 2015.

King, Josiah. *The Examination and Tryal of Old Father Christmas, together with his clearing by the Jury, at the Assizes held at the town of Difference, in the county of Discontent*. London: H Brome, T Basset and J Wright. 1678. The online transcript is from a later reprinting of 1686.

Of Russian Origin: Ded Moroz, Russiapedia. Autonomous Nonprofit Organization. 2005-2011. Web. 23 November 2015.

Simpson, Jacqueline; Roud, Steve *A Dictionary of English Folklore*. Oxford: Oxford University Press. 2000. Print.

"Czech Republic." *St. Nicholas*. Stnicholascenter.org. Web. Web. 23 November 2015.

Wikipedia contributors. "Father Christmas." *Wikipedia, The Free Encyclopedia.* Wikipedia, The Free Encyclopedia. Web. 25 Dec. 2015.

Wikipedia contributors. "Nisse (folklore)." *Wikipedia, The Free Encyclopedia.* Wikipedia, The Free Encyclopedia. Web. 23 Dec. 2015.

Wikipedia contributors. "Yule Goat." *Wikipedia, The Free Encyclopedia.* Wikipedia, The Free Encyclopedia. Web. 16 Dec. 2015.

Wikipedia contributors. "Yule Lads." *Wikipedia, The Free Encyclopedia.* Wikipedia, The Free Encyclopedia, 22 Dec. 2016. Web. 22 Dec. 2015.

WEIRD SANTA PHOTOS

It is amazing the many ways Santa has been portrayed in photographs and illustrations throughout time. Check out these choice photos of Santa sacrificing a turkey, playing with a voodoo doll, being fondled by children, and just being plain weird.

Please Mr. Fireman, don't chop up Santa with an axe...

Santa going cray with the wassail...

Wait, a turkey drawn sleigh?

Umm, those eyes—is Santa on drugs or about to explode in a murderous rage?

Is Santa sacrificing a turkey?

Death by Santa—I guess that's one way to go.

Why is Santa being groped
by little girls and boys?

Who knew Santa played
with Voodoo dolls?

That's it, Santa, you're fired!

SILENT NIGHT

USING THE DARK PART OF THE YEAR TO BRIGHTEN YOUR LIFE

by Morgan St. Knight

Have you run out of holiday cheer? When you hear people singing "fa-la-la", do you think of another "F" word? Have you secretly contemplated replacing Baby Jesus with Baby Cthulu in the local church's Nativity scene just to release some pent-up hostility?

You're not Scrooge. Not yet, anyway. You'd be surprised how many people are faking their way through the holiday scene just to keep up appearances. It's no wonder. This is the time of year when the days are getting shorter and just about everywhere in the Northern Hemisphere the weather is getting colder. This is a time that's perfect for introspection, for planning, and for resting to renew our strength before spring.

Do we get to do that? No. We're bombarded with tinsel, Christmas trees and the Jolly Old Elf in every store we enter as soon as the last echo of "Trick or Treat" fades. We're also bombarded with images of shopping, shopping, shopping and spending, spending, spending pressure which may cause us to waste way more money than we can afford. Those commercials showing people gathered around a tree opening gifts don't help either, and can be especially painful for those who can't afford that extravagance.

There's one thing we all have access to, regardless of our bank accounts. It's the special energy that this part of the year brings. It's the energy of ebbing, of fading away. Rather than be depressed by this, seize the opportunity to make needed changes in your life.

If depression is one of the things you need to change this is a perfect time to tackle it, along with all of the other detritus you want out of your life. This ritual is best done right before the winter solstice. This year the solstice falls on a Sunday, so doing this on the previous Saturday night would be perfect if you hold with planetary influences, since Saturn is a planet of binding.

Take a large black candle—seven-day if you can get one—and anoint it with a bodily fluid. In my work I prefer to use my blood, but you can use any fluid you choose. The candle represents you and your power to destroy and/or eliminate what you no longer desire in your life.

Write all of the things you want out of your life on a piece of paper. It can be depression, doubt, fear, self-sabotage, poverty (of mind, body and spirit as well as bank account) or any other influence you want out of your life. You may use several small pieces of paper if you prefer, one for each thing you want gone. If you've used one larger piece of paper, fold it away from you, turn it 90 degrees counterclockwise (so what was the left edge is now facing you) and fold again. Do this two more times. Light the candle, pierce the paper with a large knife (preferably one that is NOT all metal, since you don't want to add nasty burns to the list of things you don't want in your life anymore) and hold the knife in the candle flame. As it burns, state your intention that these things you have named will be removed from your life. You can use this to remove people, too. If you have written these things or people on several smaller pieces of paper, pierce as many as you can with the knife and put it in the flame. Repeat as needed until all of the slips of paper are burned.

Save the ashes and place them under the candle. When the candle has burned out, take the ashes to a body of running water and toss them in. Place beautiful things in the empty candle jar. You may use glass stones from a craft store, natural stones, or a mix, perhaps adding a few semi-precious stones like amethyst or rose quartz if you like, or you can just use it as a vase to hold flowers. You can also fill it three quarters of the way with soil and place a bulb inside, covering with a little more soil but leaving the top third exposed. You can use tulips, daffodils, paper whites, etc. Allow the bulb to bloom. Be careful with watering though, as the glass candle casing has no drainage hole. Overwatering could cause the bulb to rot, which it the opposite of what you want to do. Keep the glass where you can see it daily to remind you of your ability to remove unwanted things in your life and replace them with things of beauty, things you like.

For some practitioners, the turning of the solar tides on and just after the winter solstice means darkness is giving way to light. The idea that a new year has arrived, along with the promise of new beginnings, is a powerful image made even more powerful by the intentions of millions of people who truly believe it. So it's a perfect time to tap into that collective energy to bring needed changes in your life.

Two entities who are perfect for this are Chango and Oya-Iansa. Both have control over fire, which is not only ever-changing but also clears away old debris so new things can grow. Both are also fierce warriors who can help you find your courage so you can make needed changes in your life. Be careful though. Fire burns, and you must control it, which means you must do your part to ensure a successful working. They will help your fiercely, but they won't do the job for you.

To call on Chango for the courage you need to enact change in your life and meet new challenges, get a red seven-day candle. If you're inclined to use saints in your work, St. Barbara and St. Michael are two often associated with him. Gather four bananas, four red apples, four red pears and four red plums (you may substitute four pomegranates for one of the fruits). Place them in bowls or on clean dishes. Lay the containers on the floor then light the candle and place it in between the dishes. Ask Chango for the courage to meet your challenges and confidence to go into any battle you may face in the coming year. After four days have passed, gather the fruits, put them into a brown paper bag, and leave it at the foot of an oak tree with four pennies. If an oak tree is not available or convenient, any large tree will do.

Oya-Iansa will also help you with battles, but she is especially helpful when you need to bring change into your life. Whether you need to break a bad habit or to simply change your life in general, she's the one to go to. But be careful, because if you are not specific about how much change you are ready to accept she could upend your life entirely. It will ultimately be to your benefit, but if you have certain things, activities, or people you want to keep, make sure you tell her!

Get nine small eggplants. Chinese eggplants work, but if you have an Asian or Indian market in your area check them. They often have baby eggplants that are the perfect size for this ritual.

Place them on a platter or in a bowl. Place a shiny penny in between the individual eggplants, using a total of nine pennies. Drizzle a good oil over the slices, making sure to coat the pennies too. Traditionally palm oil is used, but there's no need to get a whole container of it if you only plan to use it for one ritual. You can use good olive oil instead. A chili oil, such as you can find in the Asian section of the grocery store, will also work (and you can use the rest in your own recipes, so it's not too wasteful). Oya-Iansa likes her food like she likes her lovers—spicy!

Again, you'll need one of the larger glass-encased candles, but this one should be either a deep red or dark purple. If you work with saints, Our Lady of Candelaria or St. Theresa of Lisieux are appropriate. They can be somewhat hard to find, especially with a candle of the right color, so instead you can get a plain glassed candle and find a picture of either saint online, print it out, and hang it above the area where you plan to leave the offering.

Write the changes you envision (and any restrictions, as mentioned above) on a sheet of paper and place the candle over it and light it. Place the eggplants on the ground near the candle. Each morning, go to the candle and think clearly about what changes you need. Do this for nine mornings. You will probably have to get another candle and transfer the flame because the first one will go out before the nine days have passed.

On the tenth day gather the eggplants and pennies, put them in a brown paper bag and take them to a cemetery. Leave them just inside the gate, and thank Oya-Iansa for her help. If you don't like the idea of going to the cemetery, you can leave the bag in a busy marketplace (a mall would work) on a bench. Oya-Iansa controls the market as well as the cemetery. If you lit a second candle, continue to let it burn until it goes out. You do not need to do the daily meditation in front of it, but it will help if you visit it at least once a day and thank Oya-Iansa again.

Of course the master of change par excellence is Legba, also known as Ellegua. He is owner of all roads and can open or close any door he pleases, so he can certainly open the doors of opportunity for you and close the doors to worries and cares.

Ideally he is invoked before any other interaction with an entity such as Chango or Oya-Iansa, so if you want to cover your bases, light a white votive candle to him before you perform the rituals to ask them for help. A small glass of rum and a cigar will go over well with him too.

To ask him to clear your path of obstacles and burdens (or, in other terms, to ask him to close the door on those unwanted things) and to open the path to opportunities and good fortune, you can cook him a meal of chicken, beans and rice, and some nice (peeled) orange sections. If you can find cassava bread add that too, as he is said to be very fond of it. Otherwise you can place three nice crusty pieces of French bread on top of the beans and rice.

Get a seven day candle for him. You have some leeway with colors here. White is always appropriate when working with Legba, You can also find candles that are half red, half black, which are the two primary colors associated with him. If you work with saints, a candle for St. Peter, St. Lazarus, St. Martin of Porres, or the Infant of Prague or Niño Atocha would be appropriate.

Pour three small glasses of rum and place them and the food on the floor, with the candle among the plates. Light the candle and ask Legba for what you need. Allow the food to sit for three days, then pack it in brown paper bags (you should double up the one that has the rice and beans). Pour the rum into the earth somewhere, and leave the bag at a crossroads along with three pennies. Let the candle continue burning in your home until it goes out.

It is very, very important in working with any of the spells involving entities is to thank them when your favors are received. If the favor is unfolding over a period of time, such as having courage for a battle, making big changes, or improving your circumstances in general, don't wait until everything is done. Go ahead and give them a thank you as it's happening. With some entities, like St. Expedite and the Dead, you should wait until the favor is absolutely granted before giving them thank you offerings, or they may think you're satisfied and stop mid-job. In the case of lwa and orisha, it never hurts to show gratitude early on. To do this you can get another candle like the one you offered in the ritual and burn it in their honor.

If they come through in a really big way, especially with a result that was beyond your dreams, then it is a good idea to throw them a party, inviting friends who will at least be sympathetic to, if not sharing outright, your beliefs. Make sure everyone knows you are throwing the party in honor of the entity who helped you. If your blessings didn't include enough cash to throw an outright fete, you can cook them a thank-you meal similar to the one you offered them before, only this time serve yourself some of the food on the plate, sit down with the offerings, and eat while offering thanks for getting blessings.

Never forget that these rituals can be done any time you need. You don't have to wait until this time of year. But a wise practitioner never says "no" to a little extra help, and if you can tap into the energies that are flowing around the winter solstice, you could get enough of a boost to turn a simple wish into a very big dream come true.

HOLY DAY HOODOO

By Carolina Dean

Gingerbread men figure candles. Photo courtesy of Carolina Dean.

Looking at these cute gingerbread men candles; it may never have occurred to you that you could use them in the same way as regular old human figure candles. Figure candles are those candles which have been molded in the shape of a male or female figure and are often used to represent a specific person. They come in various colors including black, white, green, and red. Just as in general candle burning practices, the color of the candle should be in harmony with the goal of your spell.

Typically, the name of the person the candle is intended to represent is scratched across the chest of the figure candle. The individual's personal concerns, when available, are loaded into the base of the candle. Once prepared, the candle may be burned either alone or with other candles. These types of candles can just as easily be used in the same manner as a waxen image because that is exactly what they are!

To prepare such a candle as a doll-baby, you can simply scratch the person's name across the chest of the doll. If you have personal concerns, or wish to incorporate herbs and roots into your doll, the candle will have to be loaded. To load the candle, bore a hole in the bottom and fill this with your herbs, personal concerns, and so forth and then fill the hole back in with wax to seal it. In the case of the candles pictured on the previous page, I would more than likely scrape off the outer layer of decoration and wipe them down with ammonia to cleanse them before using them in any such spell.

With this idea in mind, let's look at some other items you would typically find in the home during the holidays and how you use them in magical ways.

Mistletoe is traditionally hung about the home, usually just inside doorways, and anyone caught standing under it is kissed. There are many different theories associated with the origin of this practice but most agree that it has to do with bestowing fertility and protection. In the hoodoo tradition, Mistletoe can be dried, powdered and mixed with Verbena and Elecampane to make a love powder. When burned with Oak Wood and Rue, it drives away evil and mistletoe makes a good addition to any mojo bag or herb packet for love or healing.

Live Pine Trees often act as Christmas Trees and their needles can be saved and used in recipes for baths and floor washes to spiritually cleanse the home. Pine needles are also used in workings to draw in money, drive out evil spirits, and remove negativity.

There are many things that you can do with holiday cards which are both given and received. Whenever I receive holiday cards I always make it a point to gently tear off the portion of the envelope where the sender signed his or her name and address. These can be placed under candles, in dolls, or mojo bags as personal concerns. Before you send out your own cards I always suggest: a) printing your return address from your computer, and

b) using a moist sponge to seal the envelope rather than licking it and giving away your own personal concerns so easily. In addition, your cards can be dusted with hoodoo powders or smoked in incenses to have an effect on the receiver for good or bad. For example, you can dip the four corners in powdered sugar so that the card will be received with affection. Just be sure to blow off any excess powder so the person you send it to won't be suspicious.

Christmas stockings usually hung over the fireplace for Santa to put smaller gifts and treats can be used in the same manner as a person's sock. In many cases, they also have the person's name embroidered on them. Let's say that your boyfriend broke up with you right before Christmas or your mother-in-law swore she would never come to your house again since you didn't name the new baby after her father and you want to Hot Foot him or her away for good. Take the person's Christmas stocking and stuff some dried hot peppers, powdered red pepper, black pepper, and their personal concerns down in the toe. Next, beginning at the toe roll the stocking away from you making your prayer or petition for them to go away. Tie up the stocking with some cord or thread (you probably have some left over ribbon somewhere) and toss it in your burning fire place to really light a fire under them! Alternately, if you have a family member who will be absent or traveling during the holidays you can put items down in the toe of their stocking such as Peony (for protection) or Comfrey Root (safe travel).

Gift wrapping paper can often be found all over the house on Christmas morning, especially if you have small children or childish adults! I know many people who try to tear their paper off carefully so it can be reused but for our purposes this isn't necessary. Gift wrapping paper, especially those in solid colors (green, blue, pink, etc.), can be saved and used to tie up herbal packets along with any leftover ribbon. As far as possible, try to coordinate the color of the paper to your goal. For example green paper and gold ribbon for a money herb packet. In addition, smaller pieces can be saved for writing your petition papers on the reverse side (which is usually white).

Holly wreaths can often be seen on doors and over mantles this time of year and this is a holdover from Northern Europe when Holly was hung on doors and windows to prick evil spirits and keep them out of the home. Holly is also considered very lucky for men and so a Holly leaf can be hidden in a man's suit or coat pocket for protection and good luck. When the holidays are over, three leaves from a Holly wreath can be placed behind the sill over doors and window for continued protection.

There are many things that can be done with tree ornaments. For example, those that take the form of humans (and animals) can be used in the same manner as a doll baby. Before hanging them on the tree, name them after family members and anoint them with Peace Oil so that your holiday will go off without any family squabbles. In addition, those shiny ball ornaments can be utilized as a temporary reverse mirror box to keep friends and family safe through the holidays. Just write out your petition paper and fold it around a protective root, such as Peony, and slip it inside the ornamental ball. To do this, you will have to gently remove the hook and then glue it back on.

Children the world over often put out cookies and milk for Santa, but you don't have to be a child to petition the "real" Saint Nicholas who is known as the patron Saint of children, sailors, fishermen, merchants, broadcasters, the falsely accused, repentant thieves, pharmacists, archers, pawnbrokers, and prostitutes. He can be petitioned for prosperity, protection (especially sailors, business owners, and prostitutes) as well as for general wishes. To petition Saint Nicholas you can simply light a candle next to a Santa Claus figurine (we'll know who it *really* represents, won't we?). It won't hurt to put out milk and cookies either. To honor the spirit of Saint Nicholas or thank him for his blessings, make an anonymous donation to a charity that benefits children or buy a toy for a child whose parents cannot afford to buy him or her anything.

Speaking of cookies, there are all kinds of holiday-foods that can be used in a magical way to bring you success, money, love, and more. Gingerbread men cookies can be used in the same manner as a doll baby. Got an enemy you want to get rid of? Name a gingerbread man cookie after him and break off one piece a day for several days. Crush the piece to a powder and leave it at a crossroads. Do this every day for 13 days as the moon wanes. Want to draw a lover to you? Name one cookie after yourself and another after your lover (or simply "my lover") and bind them together with red ribbon. Place them in a special box (maybe one of those boxes that Christmas chocolates come in) and sprinkle it with cinnamon, sugar, and ginger. Need money? Sprinkle a little cinnamon powder over a pecan pie in the shape of a dollar sign as you make your petition. As you eat the pie, imagine your bank account becoming as fat as your Aunt Ethel! Finally, don't forget to save those turkey bones to conjure up some fowl magic!

Finally, if you grew up in a Christian household at one point or another someone probably sat you down and read the story of the Nativity to you. This was usually done before bed on Christmas Eve to teach the children the true meaning of Christmas. In light of all the dangers going on in the world right now, I suggest that at some point during the week before Christmas you take a few moments to sit quietly and meditate on *Luke Chapter 20*. Pay special attention to verses 40 and 52 and make this wish for all the children of the world. If you are a parent, you may wish to anoint your own children with Holy Oil while praying these verses to that they grow strong in spirit and filled with wisdom and the love of God.

Happy Holy Days!

IMAGE CREDITS

Gumbo Ya Ya incorporates images that are licensed under Public Domain and Creative Commons designations. Any images not listed below are deemed to be licensed under Public Domain. If there are any images incorrectly attributed or not attributed that are under copyright, no violation is intended and the publisher requests correct information be sent to the editor so that a proper attribution may be given in subsequent printings.

P. 13 Schenkman, Jan. *St. Saint Nicholas and his servant.* 1850. Illustration. *Sint Nikolaas en zijn Knecht.* Licensed under Public Domain via Wikimedia Commons.

P. 17 *Old Father Christmas*, Forrester's Pictorial Miscellany for the Family Circle (1854). Licensed under Public Domain via Wikimedia Commons.

P. 24 Official poster for the movie *Krampus: The Reckoning.* 2015. Fun House Features. Web. 22 November 2015. Fair use.

P. 25 Official poster for the movie *A Christmas Horror Story.* 2015. Copperheart Entertainment. Web. 22 November 2015. Fair use.

P. 25 Official poster for the film *Krampus The Christmas Devil*. 2014. Snowdog Studio. Web. 22 November 2015. Fair use.

P. 26 Official poster for the film *Night of the Krampus*. 2013. Fighting Owl Films. Web. 22 November 2015. Fair use.

P. 26 Official poster for the film *Silent Night Bloody Night 2: Revival*. 2015. 42nd Street Films. Web. 22 November 2015. Fair use.

P. 27 Official poster for the film *Santa Krampus*. Wormwood Studios. Web. 22 November 2015. Fair use.

P. 28 Long, Carolyn M. *Gloria in Excelsis Deo*. 2015. Illustration. Used with permission.

P. 30 Long, Carolyn M. *Welcome Yule*. 2014. Illustration. Used with permission.

P. 33 Hodan, George. *Baking*. Photograph. *Public Domain Pictures*. Bobek Ltd. Web. 22 November 2015. Licensed under Public Domain.

P. 43 Nankivell, Frank. A. *Santa Claus.* 1902. *Puck* v. 52, no. 1344, 3 December 1902. Web. 21 September 2015. Licensed under Public Domain via Wikimedia Commons.

P. 46-47 Jaritz, Johann. *Krampus parade in Pörtschach am Wörthersee.* 2013. Photograph. *Wikimedia Commons.* Wikimedia Foundation, Inc. Web. 22 November 2015. Licensed under CC BY-SA 3.0.

P. 49 *Gruss vom Krampus (Greetings from Krampus).* Illustration. *Wikimedia Commons.* Wikimedia Foundation, Inc. Web. 22 November 2015. Licensed under Public Domain via Wikimedia Commons.

P. 51 *Krampus and St. Nicolas.* Illustration. *Wikimedia Commons.* Wikimedia Foundation, Inc. Web. 22 November 2015. Licensed under Public Domain via Wikimedia Commons.

P. 52 Martinez, Anita. *Perchtenlauf Klagenfurt.* 2006. Photograph. *Wikimedia Commons.* Wikimedia Foundation, Inc. Web. 22 November 2015. Licensed under CC BY-SA 3.0 at via Commons.

P. 55 Kabel, Matthias *A person dressed as Krampus at Morzger Pass, Salzburg (Austria).* Photograph. *Wikimedia Commons.* Wikimedia Foundation, Inc.

Web. 22 November 2015. Licensed under Own work, copyleft: Multi-license with GFDL and Creative Commons CC-BY-SA-2.5 and older versions (2.0 and 1.0).

P. 56-57 Šubic, Jurij. *Jurij Šubic - Nikolo.* Illustration. *Wikimedia Commons.* Wikimedia Foundation, Inc. Web. 22 November 2015. Licensed under Public Domain via Wikimedia Commons.

P. 58 *Nikolaus und Krampus.* Illustration. *Wikimedia Commons.* Wikimedia Foundation, Inc. Web. 22 November 2015. Licensed under Public Domain via Wikimedia Commons.

P. 60 Bilibin, Ivan. *Ded Moroz.* 1932. Illustration. *Wikimedia Commons.* Wikimedia Foundation, Inc. Web. 22 November 2015. This work is in the public domain in Russia according to article 1281 of Book IV of the Civil Code of the Russian Federation No. 230-FZ of December 18, 2006 and article 6 of Law No. 231-FZ of the Russian Federation of December 18, 2006 (the Implementation Act for Book IV of the Civil Code of the Russian Federation).

P. 63 *Father Christmas.* 1879. Illustration. *Fun.* London, England. Issue 763, 24 December 1879, p 256. Web. 22 November 2015. Licensed under Public Domain via Wikimedia Commons.

P. 65 Almanach de Wintzenheim. *Hans Trapp.* Photograph. *Wikimedia Commons.* Wikimedia Foundation, Inc. Web. 22 November 2015. Licensed under CC BY-SA 3.0 via Wikimedia Commons.

P. 70-71 Bauer, John. *Julnatten.* 1913. Illustration. *Among Gnomes and Trolls. WikiArt.* Wikiart.org. Web. 25 November 2015. Licensed under Public Domain via WikiArt.

P. 74 Seymour, Robert. *Folk depiction of Father Christmas riding on a goat.* 1888. Illustration. *The Book of Christmas. Wikimedia Commons.* Wikimedia Foundation, Inc. Web. 25 November 2015. Licensed under Public Domain via Wikimedia Commons.

P. 77 Bauer, John. *Jultomten* 1911. Illustration. *Among Gnomes and Trolls. WikiArt.* Wikiart.org. Web. 25 November 2015. Licensed under Public Domain via WikiArt.

P. 81 Knecht Ruprecht und das Christkind. 19th century. Illustration. *Wikimedia Commons.* Wikimedia Foundation, Inc. Web. 22 October 2015. Licensed under Public Domain via Wikimedia Commons.

P. 85 Rosen, George von. *Odin, the Wanderer.* 1886. Illustration. Appeared in the 1893 Swedish translation of the *Poetic Edda*. *Wikimedia Commons*. Wikimedia Foundation, Inc. Web. 22 November 2015. Licensed under Public domain via Wikimedia Commons.

P. 93 Vasnetsov, Viktor M. *Vasnetsov Snegurochka*. Illustration. Scanned from *A. K. Lazuko Victor Vasnetsov*, Leningrad: Khudozhnik RSFSR. 1990. Licensed under Public Domain via Wikimedia Commons.

P. 97 Baltica. *Swedish Gävle goat (Gävlebocken)*. Photograph. *Wikimedia Commons*. Wikimedia Foundation, Inc. Web. 22 November 2015. Licensed under Public Domain via Wikimedia Commons.

P. 102 *Santa Claus Story*. 1921. Photograph. Publisher unknown. *Library of Congress*. Library of Congress Prints and Photographs Division, Washington, D.C. Web. 22 November 2015. Rights Advisory: No known restrictions on publication.

P. 104 Crawford, Will. *Hands up!* 1912. Illustration. Keppler & Schwarzmann, New York. *Library of Congress*. Library of Congress Prints and Photographs Division, Washington, D.C. Web. 22 November 2015. Rights Advisory: No known restrictions on publication.

P. 104 *Father Christmas Not Up-To-Date. 1897.* Punch, Almanac for 1897. Wikimedia Commons. Wikimedia Foundation, Inc. Web. 22 November 2015. Licensed under Public Domain via Wikimedia Commons.

P. 105 *Santa Claus on NEW YORK.* Photograph. Bain News Service. *Library of Congress.* Library of Congress Prints and Photographs Division, Washington, D.C. Web. 22 November 2015. Rights Advisory: No known restrictions on publication.

P. 105 Kilburn, Benjamin, W. *Santa Captured.* 1897. Photograph. *Library of Congress.* Library of Congress Prints and Photographs Division, Washington, D.C. Web. 22 November 2015. Rights Advisory: No known restrictions on publication.

P. 116 Harris, Dean. *Gingerbread Men Figure Candles.* 2015. Digital Photo. Used by permission.

CONTRIBUTORS

My heartfelt gratitude is given to each of our contributors for their time and generosity.

Denise Alvarado

Denise Alvarado (1960) was born and raised in the rich Creole culture of New Orleans, Louisiana. She has studied indigenous healing traditions from a personal and academic perspective for over four decades. She is the author of numerous books about Southern folk traditions, including *The Conjurer's Guide to St. Expedite, The Voodoo Hoodoo Spellbook,* the *Hoodoo Almanacs, The Voodoo Doll Spellbook, Voodoo Dolls in Magick and Ritual* and more. She is the Editor in Chief of *Gumbo Ya Ya,* the *Hoodoo Almanacs* and the *Journal of American Rootwork.* Her provocative artwork has been featured on several television shows including *National Geographic's Taboo, The Originals,* and *Blue Bloods.* She is a rootworker in the Louisiana tradition, a spiritual artist, and teacher of southern conjure at Crossroads University, crossroadsuniversity.com. Visit her websites: creolemoon.com and voodoomuse.org for a little sweet tea and conjure.

Bayou Basil
You can find Bayou Basil at: bayoubasil.wix.com/bayoubasil or email bayoubasil@gmail.com. She can be found on Facebook at: facebook.com/bayoubasil

Carole Cusack
Carole M. Cusack is Professor of Religious Studies at the University of Sydney. She trained as a medievalist and author of *Invented Religions: Imagination, Fiction and Faith* (Ashgate 2010), *The Sacred Tree: Ancient and Medieval Manifestations* (Cambridge Scholars 2011) and *Anime, Religion and Spirituality: Profane and Sacred Worlds in Contemporary Japan* (with Katharine Buljan, Equinox 2015). Since the late 1990s she has taught in contemporary religious trends, publishing on pilgrimage and tourism, modern Pagan religions, new religious movements, and religion and popular culture.

Carolina Dean
Born and raised in South Carolina, Rev. Carolina Dean is a modern Two-Headed Doctor in the Southern Folk Magic Tradition. He is the co-author of the *Hoodoo Almanac 2012* through 2015, as well as a frequent contributor to and Assistant Editor of *Hoodoo and Conjure Magazine.* As a Reader, a Rootworker, and a Magical Craftsman, he offers a wide variety of goods and services including Custom Mo-

jo Bags, Setting of Lights, Tarot Readings, and Custom Doll Babies (for which he is widely known). As an ordained minister, he occasionally performs religious and spiritual ceremonies such as weddings, funerals, baby-blessings and house-blessings. As an openly gay man, he is especially sensitive to the needs of the LGBT community. Learn more about Dean by visiting his website: carolinaconjure.com.

Celeste Heldstab
Celeste Heldstab is the author of of *Llewellyn's Complete Formulary of Magical Oils* and owns Bayou Witch Incense LLC at bayouwitchincense.com. She is an herbalist, "perfumista" (collector of fine perfumes from around the world) and dabbles in crafting Artisan perfumes, magical oils, and incense and has been in business for over 20 years.

Mama Moon
Debbe, aka Mama Moon, was trained as a traditional witch and herbalist by her mother. She received her certification in herbal medicine in 2002. Debbe currently lives in Chicago and runs Crescent Moon Herb and Conjure and can be found on Facebook: facebook.com/Crescent-Moon-Herb-Conjure-1498874403694778

Melony Malsom
An artist and writer for over 20 years, Melony enjoys creating and selling encaustic pieces and her

Evil Twin Conjure Products on Etsy. Melony is currently working on several writing and artistic endeavors, including an easy reference guide to the Lwa. **Facebook:** facebook.com/melony.malsom

Morgan St. Knight
Morgan St. Knight lives in Atlanta where she has practiced Southern Hoodoo and New Orleans-style Voodoo for more than 30 years. She is also the author of the urban fantasy novel *Curse of Prometheus: a tale of Medea*, and her website is talesofmedea.com.

To Our Readers

Creole Moon Publications is a small independent publisher specializing in the cultural and spiritual traditions and folklore of the American South. Our mission is to publish quality books that observe and preserve southern cultural heritage and folk magic traditions that will make a difference in people's lives. We value the integrity, originality, and depth of knowledge of our authors.

Our readers are our most important resource, and we appreciate your input, suggestions, and ideas about what you would like to see published.

Visit our website at *www.creolemoon.com* to learn about our upcoming books and downloads, join our Conjure Club, and to sign up for newsletters and exclusive offers.

You can also contact us at creolemoonpublications@gmail.com or at:

Creole Moon Publications
P.O. Box 25687
Prescott Valley, AZ. 86312

CREOLE MOON'S CONJURE CLUB

FOR THE SERIOUS STUDENT OF SOUTHERN CONJURE

If you are an information seeker, an academic interested in the inner workings of southern conjure traditions, or a practitioner of conjure yourself, you will love our Conjure Club. Each month you will receive on the average 3 to 4 digital downloads and ebooks full of information about traditional conjure workings, working with Catholic saints and folk saints, information about herbs and roots, conjure formularies, various spirits found on the altars of rootworkers all over the South, how to work with lamps, graveyard work, bottle spells, money magic, love spells and much, much more! For more information, please visit:

www.conjureclub.com

CREOLE MOON PUBLICATIONS

TITLE	PRICE
333 Conjure Tips and Tricks By Denise Alvarado and Madrina Angelique	$9.00
Conjure Diary By Denise Alvarado, Carolina Dean, Alyne Pustanio	$13.00
The Conjure Digest Vol 1 By Denise Alvarado	$9.00
Conjuring Black Hawk By Denise Alvarado	$24.95
Crossroads Mamas 105 Spiritual Baths for Every Occasion By Denise Alvarado and Madrina Angelique	$13.00
Day of the Dead Handbook By Denise Alvarado	$13.00
Fortune Telling with Playing Cards By P.R.S. Foli	$7.95
Gumbo Ya Ya #3	$9.00
Gumbo Ya Ya #4	$9.00
Gumbo Ya Ya #5	$9.00
Gumbo Ya Ya All Hallow's Eve	$9.00
Gumbo Ya Ya Hallowe'en 2015	$9.00
Gumbo Ya Ya Krampus-Santa Issue	$13.00
Gypsy Wisdom, Spells Charms and Folklore By Denise Alvarado	$13.00
Hoodoo Almanac 2012 By Denise Alvarado, Carolina Dean and Alyne Pustanio	$19.95
Hoodoo Almanac 2013 Gazette By Denise Alvarado, Carolina Dean and Alyne Pustanio	$19.95
Hoodoo Almanac 2014 & 2015 (2 years) By Denise Alvarado, Carolina Dean and Alyne Pustanio	$19.95
Hoodoo and Conjure Quarterly Premiere Issue By Multiple authors, Denise Alvarado, Editor/Contributor	$44.95
Hoodoo and Conjure Quarterly #2 By Multiple authors, Denise Alvarado, Editor/Contributor	$24.95
Hoodoo and Conjure New Orleans By Multiple authors, Denise Alvarado, Editor/Contributor	$24.95
Hoodoo and Conjure New Orleans 2014 By Multiple authors, Denise Alvarado, Editor/Contributor	$24.95
Journal of American Rootwork Vol. 1 Denise Alvarado, Editor	$25.00
Purloined Stories and Early Tales of Old New Orleans By Alyne Pustanio	$15.95
Secrets of a Sissy Boy By Carolina Dean	$19.95
The True Grimoire By King Solomon	$7.95
Voodoo Dolls in Magick and Ritual By Denise Alvarado	$19.95
Workin' in da Boneyard By Denise Alvarado and Madrina Angelique	$13.00

ORDER FORM

TITLE	QUANTITY	SUBTOTAL
	Order Subtotal	
	Tax	
	Shipping	
	Total	

Two ways to order

Complete the order form and choose one of the following methods to place your order.

Order Online:

Visit our website creolemoonpublications.com, select your books and order them on our secure server.

Order by Mail:

Shipping is $6.75 for the first title and $2.00 for each additional title. International shipping is $9.15 per title. Please make your check or money order out to "Denise Alvarado". Send the full price of your order (AZ residents add 7.35% sales tax) in U.S funds plus postage and handling to: Creole Moon, P.O. Box 25687, Prescott Valley, AZ 86312.